Biblical Dynamics for Revival Today

Lessons from the Life of King Hezekiah

Second Edition

Dr. Raphael J. Thomas

Foreword by Dr. William "Billy" Hall

ISBN: 1-4392-7503-3
ISBN-13: 9781439275030

Book Design and Typesetting by Raphael Thomas

Printed by
Create Space

Dedication

To my wife, Velda,
And my sons,
Timothy and Nathanael.
You have been a source
of inspiration, motivation and encouragement.

To the memory of my parents
Frederick and Fay Thomas (deceased).
I appreciate the investment that they made in my life.

To all who are fervently praying for revival
in our time. May this book fuel the fire until we see
the glory of God manifested.

TABLE OF CONTENTS

ACKNOWLEDGEMENTS

First of all I give thanks to God for His direction to write this book. I was acutely aware of His divine illumination as I prepared the messages that form the basis of this book. I was also aware of the opposition of the Enemy, in various ways, to prevent the writing of this book. Indeed, the conclusion of this is testimony to the fact that God has won the battle another time. To God be the glory! He causes us to triumph! To Him I give supreme thanks.

At the earthly level, I give thanks to my wife, Velda, and my two sons: Timothy and Nathanael. Although I tried to write this book in what could be considered 'spare time,' there were occasions when my mind was so captivated by the contents of the book that I became momentarily cut off from my family. During those moments they, nevertheless, showed understanding and gave support, love and encouragement. Indeed, they have provided inspiration and motivation for me. They have proved themselves to be truly the spice in my life.

I also thank my family of origin, beginning with my parents Frederick and Fay Thomas. They always went the extra mile to care for all their children. They have done a great job in facilitating the call of God on my life. And along with them I thank my sister Veronica; my brothers Donovan, Derrick, Byron and my cousin

Clifton. All of them have played an invaluable part in helping me to grow up in a loving and healthy family environment, as well as encouraging me along with this project.

Also, I thank the many organizations and institutions that have made significant impressions on my life. These include Jamaica Youth for Christ (JYFC), Schools Christian Fellowship/Scripture Union (SCF/SU), Jamaica Theological Seminary (JTS), Caribbean Graduate School of Theology (CGST), United Theological College of the West Indies (UTCWI), Columbia Theological Seminary (CTS), Haggai Institute (HI) and Central Christian University (CCU). In addition to these, I would like to recognize the tremendous role that the Annotto Bay Gospel Chapel and the North-Eastern Missionary Conference (NEMCO) have played in my spiritual formation and leadership development.

Thanks to all our personal intercessors that have stood with us in prayer. Those prayers helped to overcome the oppositions and hindrances to the production of this book.

Thanks also to Paul and Megan Klouse who served as short term missionaries at Annotto Bay Gospel Chapel while I was writing this book.

Thanks to Jamaica Theological Seminary, Kingston Keswick Convention, and the churches in Jamaica and overseas that provided opportunity for me to share with them the messages in this book. Each presentation helped to refine these messages. The encouragement to put these messages in print largely came as a response to preaching these messages.

I also thank Dr. Billy Hall, a mentor and former instructor, for writing the foreword to this book and for serving as my consulting editor.

Thanks also to the following organizations which have contributed to my personal support and/or ministry while writing this book: Swallowfield Chapel and Christian Missions (Kingston, Jamaica), Jacksonville Chapel (New Jersey), Team Health Care (New Jersey), and Abundant Life Chiropractic (New Jersey).

FOREWORD

"Revival" is a term much used but rarely explained. This book is dedicated to make clear the concept and achieves that purpose with remarkable clarity.

The approach chosen is a detailed study of the life and times of Judah's King Hezekiah, who was used of God to lead what may be justifiably regarded as the greatest revival in Biblical or subsequent history.

Focussing on this unique revival, the author abstracts instructive, timeless truths, then applies them imaginatively and persuasively to our everyday realities and situations.

In the process of identifying, revealing, and applying those principles that Hezekiah followed, the author inspires us to seek revival in our personal lives, and, progressively, in wider spheres, until nationally, even internationally.

As the author makes his case, the lessons are clear. Yet, beyond the helpful delineations, definitions and declarations, there is a heart-felt challenge that emerges. That challenge is to apply the abstracted lessons with a burning, passionate, perseverance.

In so doing, the author succeeds in transmitting what may be termed a 'holy fire' that consumes rational dross and purifies, therefore, spiritual virtues. This fire is fuelled by the author's testimony of personal sanctification, through several prayer vigils and prolonged fasting.

Not surprisingly, all who have heard Dr. Raphael Thomas share these studies from the pulpit have been blessed with the 'holy fire' from Heaven through God's anointed servant.

Now that these studies have been edited and presented in print, many more persons will be able to share in the blessings of the teachings and the challenges generated.

My experience in reading this book in manuscript form is that I did feel the 'holy fire' as I read. My prayer is that as you read, you too, will experience the Holy Spirit's ministry through this testimony to God's glory.

The choice of Hezekiah's life and times is wise, for the divine account cannot be disputed, and the truths of God's Word abide forever. All who read this book will know for sure what revival means, and some may even discover personally how revival feels.

My prayer is that the Lord will use this little volume to accomplish big things for Him.

Dr. William "Billy" Hall

PREFACE

These messages were first preached as a series at the Spiritual Emphasis Week at Jamaica Theological Seminary in October 2000. Also, they were preached at the Kingston Keswick Convention in January 2001, as well as at a number of local churches. During those presentations numerous requests were received to make the notes available in print and in audiocassettes. These messages are now sent forth in print, with the prayer that the Lord will use them to prepare His people, in every place, for revival.

Each chapter of this book expounds a particular portion of Scripture. The selected Scripture portions, when taken together, are intended to capture the essence of the life of King Hezekiah. The objective is to identify some timeless principles relevant to spiritual renewal. I believe that the dynamics that precipitated revival in Hezekiah's time may also yield revival in our time, for revival time is now. Stalwart Old Testament scholar Dr. Walter Kaiser, in his book *Quest for Renewal: Personal Revival in the Old Testament*, said that

> inasmuch as revival remains the prerogative and special work of God, it will appear that the first requisite for any significant planning, praying, or writing in this area would be the study of revivals in the Bible.[1]

Hence, this urgent call for revival is thoroughly rooted in the biblical texts relating to Hezekiah's revival. These are the last days of God's witness to sinful humanity and as prophesied, God promises before His sealing of all opportunity to turn to Him, to send a mighty revival. Therefore, believers cannot afford to be asleep in these days, or to be casual and mediocre in their commitment to the Lord for, "the end of all things is at hand" (1 Peter 4:7). We are living in the last and closing days of the Church. We need, therefore, to be "redeeming the times for the days are evil" (Ephesians 5:16). And, that redeeming must be done by a spiritually alert church.

Our Lord and King is coming soon, and He is coming for a Church without spot and wrinkle. The Bride of Christ must, therefore, urgently adorn herself, for not long from now we will hear the shout, "Behold the bridegroom is coming; go out to meet him" (Matthew 25:6). As events unfold it is abundantly clear that it is high time to get ready. It is revival time. We can no longer settle for *survival*, we must pursue *revival*.

I do not speak about revival because I have experienced any great revivals, nor have I had any special knowledge about the intricacies of revival. I speak about revival because of the passion and burden that the Lord has given me for revival. This burden got even more intense after embarking on a number of forty-day fasts for personal and global revival, the most recent of which was partly in response to a call issued by Dr. Bill Bright for two million Christians to embark on forty-day fasts for national and worldwide revival[2].

I believe that this series of messages is one result of such forty-day fasts. It is my desire to experience, first hand, a genuine and authentic Holy Ghost revival in my life and in my lifetime. I want to see it for myself. It is a burden that I cannot carry alone, so by this means I share the burden with you.

Therefore, as I share this burden with you, I lovingly invite you to join God's army that is passionately praying for revival in our time. Let us hold on to the promise of the Lord that "the earth will be filled with the knowledge of the glory of the Lord, as the waters cover the sea" (Habakkuk 2:14). Let us adopt the spirit of Jacob and not let go until God blesses us (Genesis 32:26), for it is revival time.

God has promised that in the last days He will pour out His spirit on all flesh (Joel 2, Acts 2). In this mighty outpouring, young men will see visions, old men will dream dreams, sons and daughters shall prophesy, and even the handmaids and servants shall be a part of it. This last day outpouring of God's Spirit will transcend gender, age and social class.

We are in the latter part of the last days and I believe that the time is now ripe for revival. In his book *Light for the Nations: A Biblical Theology of Evangelisation,* Indian theologian Richard Bowie has made the following observation:

> The church has the propensity of "running down" in time; second generation Christians are not as lively and enthusiastic as their forbearers. In every generation and wherever the life and vitality of the church has run down the Holy spirit seeks to revive, awaken and renew believers so that

they may more effectively bear witness of Christ and win the lost. [3]

If you find that your church is "run down" and that your own spiritual life is lacking in zeal and fervency, it is time to cry out to God for revival. He will rekindle the flames and revive His work.

As I share these messages in this form, it is my humble prayer that they will awaken God's people to revival in our time, for I believe that a genuine, Holy Ghost generated and orchestrated revival is the greatest need of our time, and that it is coming.

> Let it come, O Lord, we pray Thee,
> Let the showers of blessing fall;
> We are waiting, we are waiting,
> Oh revive the hearts of all. [4]

PREFACE TO THE

SECOND EDITION

This book is once again being made available to the public, having been out of print shortly after it was first published. This second edition is presented with the same passion and urgency as the previous edition, as its message remains amazingly fresh and relevant to the times. Now, more than ever, the Christian church, not to mention the world at large, is desperately in need of a Holy Ghost orchestrated revival that must begin with the people of God who are hungry for revival.

Some minor changes have been made to this edition. Yet, these changes have been significant enough to warrant a new edition, instead of merely an impression. The most obvious change is the change of title. This book was first published under the title: *Revival: Studies in the Life of King Hezekiah* in 2004. Other changes have also been made to improve accuracy, currency and readability.

I would like to acknowledge the invaluable editorial and technical assistance of the staff of *BookSurge* and *Create Space*, companies of *Amazon.com,* in further refining this second edition and making it available for global circulation. I believe that this is in keeping with the Lord's desire to have these messages available to his people globally.

Again, these messages are sent forth with my earnest prayer that they will be used by the Lord to inspire revival, individually and collectively, locally and globally. This is not because of any skill or competence of the writer but because they are thoroughly rooted in the infallible word of God.

INTRODUCTION

This book is an urgent call for revival. It is a solemn call for God's people everywhere to prepare for revival. Moreover, it is a tool to help prepare people for a biblically based revival. This book, therefore, seeks to harness and channel the spiritual energy which is a characteristic of this post-modern era so that people may experience an authentic and biblically based revival.

The term "post-modern" is still very fluid, but it is often used to describe our current era dating back to 1989, although some scholars argue that we are now moving beyond the post-modern era. However, it is an era that is characterized by some dominant features such as fragmentation, disorganization, relativism and pluralism. According to the *Encyclopaedia Britannica* it is a movement

> characterized by broad **scepticism**, subjectivism, or relativism; a general suspicion of **reason**; and an acute sensitivity to the role of **ideology** in asserting and maintaining political and economic power.[5]

The mood of post modernity is a strong reaction to orthodoxy and absolutism. Much of the limitations and dogmatisms of the previous era (called the modern era) has been dismantled and there is now a new quest for more options. Many have become disillusioned by the failures in the scientific, philosophic and economic arenas to provide ultimate fulfilment and so there is free spirit of departure from acceptable norms, traditions, standards and procedures. Included in this is a new openness, or even rigorous pursuit, for divine intervention in our time as a means of solving our problems.

It is my conviction that, in this context, God is raising up an 'army' of people, to seek Him passionately for revival. Indeed, I believe that God desires to manifest His presence among all His people in unprecedented ways, as the second coming of Christ draws closer.

Therefore, we, the people of God, must do all we can to appropriately entertain the presence of God, and so hasten this revival. Of course, this does not mean that revival is solely dependent upon human effort. In truth, revival is a sovereign work of God, and can only be brought about by God Himself. But we also have a role. We are to seek revival. The sovereignty of God and the responsibility of humanity are the two rails that carry the revival train. Concerning the importance of these two elements Selwyn Hughes says:

> There are two rails running through Scripture—one is the sovereignty of God and the other is the responsibility of man. If you keep to just one of these rails, you end up being derailed. Those who talk only of the sovereignty of God end up minimizing the responsibility of man. Those who talk only of the responsibility of man end up minimizing the sovereignty of God. When we move along both rails,

making sure that we do not place a disproportionate emphasis on either truth, then we are more likely to arrive at sounder judgments and better conclusions.[6]

By respecting these two truths then, is how we, as God's people, must diligently do our part to prepare for what might be the final spiritual awakening that this world will experience. As we passionately and persistently seek spiritual renewal in our time and circumstances, we can profit by examining precedents in Scripture and in subsequent history. I believe that it will be instructive to examine at least one period of revival in detail to gain a greater understanding of some of the important elements of revival. I have chosen to focus on what may be described as the greatest Old Testament Revival in Scripture. This revival took place during the reign of King Hezekiah. But what really is *revival?*

According to Martin Lloyd Jones revival refers to

a period of unusual blessing and activity in the life of the Christian Church. Revival means awakening, stimulating the life, bringing it to the surface again. It happens primarily in the Church of God, and amongst believing people, and it is only secondly something that affects those that are outside also. Now this is a most important point, because this definition helps us to differentiate, once and for all, between a revival and an evangelistic campaign.

An evangelistic campaign is the Church deciding to do something with respect to those who are outside. A revival is not the Church deciding to do something and doing it. It is something that is done to the Church, something that happens to the Church. [7]

Revival is probably easier to describe than to define. J.I. Packer gives the following description of revival:

> The features of revival movements on the surface vary widely, perhaps as a result of different settings, yet indeed God appears to delight in variety. Nevertheless, at the level of deeper analysis, there are constant factors recognizable in all biblical and post-biblical revivals, whatever their historical, racial, and cultural settings. They number five, and are described below.
>
> o   Awareness of God's presence…
> o   Responsiveness to God's Word…
> o   Sensitiveness to Sin…
> o   Liveliness in Community…
> o   Fruitfulness in Testimony…[8]

Edwin Orr defines revival as

> that which produces an extraordinary burden of prayer, an unusual conviction of sin, an uncanny sense of the presence of God, resulting in repentance, confession, reconciliation, and restitution, with great concern for the salvation of sinners near at hand and far away.[9]

The word *revival* is made up of two parts: *re* (the prefix which means *again*) and *vival* (from the Latin word *vita* which means *life*). Therefore, our English word *revival* is aptly defined by the *Collins Concise Dictionary* as "an instance of returning to life or consciousness; restoration of vigour or vitality." [10]Many more definitions and descriptions of revival could have been cited but I humbly offer this working definition to capture the essences of revival: *Revival is a sovereign act of God in which the spiritual vitality of the people of God is restored and is evidenced by a fresh awareness of, and response to, the* **presence** *of God, the* **poisonousness** *of sin and the* **priority** *of God's mission in the world, beyond ordinary proportions.*

This definition underscores three basic elements that are associated with revival: the presence of God (deity), awareness of sin (depravity) and a concern for the work or mission of God (duty). Although revival begins with the church it often leads to the transformation of society for a *revived church will have a ripple effect on the society at large.* These three dimensions mentioned above may manifest themselves in many different forms and to different degrees. Some revivals may be local while others may be more global.

Some words which may be used to classify the degree of revival in order of magnitude and impact are *spiritual renewal, revival,* and *spiritual awakening.* However, regardless of how revival is defined, described, characterized or categorised, every revival must be evaluated against the infallible word of God. Hence, our concentrated focus on the biblical account of Hezekiah's revival.

As we focus on this period of spiritual renewal, and examine some selected texts of the biblical account of this period of spiritual renewal, I believe we can learn timeless principles that will enhance our quest for revival, and yield spiritual renewal in our time, and in our context.

This book, therefore, is based on a study of the revival of King Hezekiah who "began his reign with the most extensive reforms in the history of Judah."[11] He began his reign when he was twenty-five years old, and he reigned in Judah for twenty-nine years. Although he started reigning at the youthful age of 25, he demonstrated a conviction to serve God wholeheartedly. That conviction resulted in the transformation of his nation.

When Hezekiah ascended the throne his people were either in direct rebellion against God or compromising their faith in God. However, Hezekiah was committed to serving God faithfully in his generation, even if he had to be radical, not to mention revolutionary.

Hezekiah reigned at a time in his nation's history when God was relegated to the *periphery* of national life. However, Hezekiah was committed to restoring God to a place of *primacy*. As king, he was determined to move his backslidden nation from the pathetic plains of mediocrity, lukewarmness and half-hearted devotion, to the hills and mountain peaks of fervency in worship and service.

King Hezekiah inherited a nation that was given over to compromise, idolatry and submission to foreign powers. However, his passion for God, and his missionary zeal for the nations of the earth to know that the Lord Jehovah alone is God, with the right to rule over all the kingdoms of the earth (2 Kings 19:15, 19), would not allow him to maintain the *status quo*. Therefore, Hezekiah used every opportunity that God gave him while leading Judah to seek spiritual renewal. Consequently, his reign resulted in restoration, reformation and revival in the nation of Judah.

We can do well with some contemporary Hezekiahs who will stand against the current tides of moral decadence and loss of respect for the holy. This world is crying out for more disciples of Jesus who will leave the plain of casual Christianity and ascend into the hill of the Lord (Psalm 24:3) to serve Him with total allegiance. God is looking for those willing to pay the price that will affect their generation for God: more faithful leaders like Hezekiah.

The Lord needs people who seek Him with the whole heart. The Bible tells us that those who seek Him will find Him when they have sought Him with their whole heart (Jeremiah 29:13). God is not impressed with a casual quest for Him. He will reveal Himself to those who make it their deliberate preoccupation to seek Him passionately. Hezekiah was one who sought the Lord passionately, and history records the difference that he made in his generation. In 2 Chronicles 31:21 the divine record says concerning Hezekiah:

> And in every work that he began in the service of the house of God, in the law and in the commandment, to *seek his God*, he did it with all his heart. So he prospered (emphasis mine).

Hezekiah sought the Lord with all his heart. He was not a candidate to fit in the mould of mediocrity, the vein of vanity, or the trend of traditionalism. He went all out in his quest for God, even in dangerous times, and under critical, life-threatening circumstances. He counted it nothing to become vulnerable in his quest for God and godliness. He was prepared to blaze a new trail for God in his generation.

As I have studied the lives of the kings of Judah and Israel, one thing that has grabbed my attention is the frequency of the exhortation to seek the Lord. This observation tells me that those who have been raised up by God to provide leadership for His people have a solemn responsibility to seek His face passionately. Leaders cannot be contented with a casual, or superficial, relationship with God. It was King David who said: "Seek the LORD and his strength, seek his face continually" (1 Chronicles 16:11). Also, David told his son, and successor, King Solomon:

> Now set your heart and your soul to seek the LORD your God. Therefore arise and build the sanctuary of the LORD God, to bring the ark of the covenant of the LORD, and the holy articles of God into the house that is to be built for the name of the LORD (1 Chronicles 22:19) (emphasis mine).

Also, in 1 Chronicles 28:9 he says:

> As for you, my son Solomon, know the God of your father, and serve him with a loyal heart and with a willing mind: for the LORD searches all heart and understands intents of the thoughts. If you *seek Him*, he will be found of you; but if thou forsake Him, He will cast you off forever (emphasis mine).

The King of kings Himself says in 2 Chronicles 7:14:

> If my people, which are called by my name, shall humble themselves, and pray, and seek my face, and turn from their wicked ways; then will I hear from heaven, and will forgive their sin, and will heal their land (emphasis mine).

The Bible says of King Rehoboam that, "he did evil, because he did not prepare his heart to seek the Lord" (2 Chronicles 12:14).

Whether we do good or evil is proportional to how much we seek God, who will always manifest His presence powerfully through persons who seek Him with intensity; people who will not only seek *favours* from God, but who will seek the *face* of God;[12] who will not only seek the *grace*, *gifts*, and *goodness* of God, but also the *glory* of God, like Moses of old who cried out, "Please show me Your glory" (Exodus 33:18).

We have a promise from God that we shall seek Him and find Him when we do so with the whole heart (Jeremiah 29:13). Indeed, it is those who hunger and thirst after righteousness that will be filled (Matthew 5:6). When we meet the conditions, God will bless us tremendously. When King Asa came to the throne in Judah, the Spirit of God came upon Azariah, the son of Obed, to prophesy to him. Among the things that the prophet said to him is:

> The Lord is with you while you are with Him. If you *seek Him*, you will find Him; but if you forsake Him, He will forsake you (emphasis mine) (2 Chronicles 15:2).

As a result of that prophetic word, King Asa and the people of Judah entered into a covenant "to seek the Lord God of their father," and that led to a revival in Judah. Asa was one of the good Kings of Judah who led his nation into the way of the Lord. This was directly related to his choice to seek the Lord with all his heart.

By the time King Hezekiah came to the throne, he had the examples of good kings, wicked kings and mediocre kings. It was his prerogative to decide what kind of king he would be in Judah. Whatever choice he made, one thing was sure, he had to give account for his choice. The prophet expressed this plainly to King Asa, "your works shall be rewarded" (2 Chronicles 15:7). It is also true for us. Our works shall be rewarded. We cannot afford to settle for less than God's best. We will have to give account to Him some day. It is time to seek the Lord (Hosea 10:12).

Let us look at the context in which Hezekiah was raised up to exercise his leadership. King Hezekiah reigned in the time of the divided kingdoms. After the death of Solomon in 930 B.C., Israel became a divided nation. Ten tribes formed the Northern Kingdom, and it was called Israel. Two tribes, namely, Judah and Benjamin, formed the Southern Kingdom. It was called Judah. Hezekiah was a king of the Southern Kingdom, Judah.

When Hezekiah came to the throne in the year 715 B.C., he immediately had to face a major international challenge. The super power at the time, Assyria, was dominating the whole Fertile Crescent. Assyria was in the midst of a rapid expansion and domination programme.

Damascus was conquered by the then king of Assyria, Tiglath Pilesar III, in 732 B.C. and Samaria was conquered by the King Shalmaneser in 723/22 B.C.[13] Sargon the II, the next king of Assyria, conquered Ashdod in 711 B.C.[14] During this time of Assyria's rapid expansion, many of the smaller nations entered into a vassalage, or friendship, with Assyria. Hezekiah's father, King Ahaz, found it expedient to establish a diplomatic friendship with Assyria, for, as it is often said, 'if we cannot beat them, we join them.' However, when Hezekiah came to the throne, he did not find such a relationship glorifying to God, and so he took the risk to sever it, and face the repercussions. Whatever it cost him, Hezekiah was determined to let his reign glorify God.

He certainly came to the throne in challenging times, but that did not cause him to compromise his religious convictions. The nation was at a low ebb spiritually, morally and economically. But, so often when there is chaos and tragedy, people are better prepared for God's intervention. Revival often comes on the heel of tragedy, which seems to have a way of causing people to think about ultimate issues. It is not surprising, then, that there was a greater interest in the things of God after the September eleven (9/11) attack on America in 2001. Sometimes, the tragedies of life help us to give God our undivided attention. Challenging times challenge people to seek God.

It was in challenging times that Hezekiah was called upon to lead his backslidden nation back to God. I am convinced that if we follow the same principles that Hezekiah followed, we too, will have the joy of experiencing personal revival, as well as revival in our various contexts in these challenging times, for "while structure and methodologies may change, principles remain constant in every age and culture."[15] It is revival time.

God is waiting to manifest His presence in the midst of the moral decadence and spiritual wickedness of our time. As God did in Hezekiah's day, God will again do through those who seek Him today with a burning passion that is almost insatiable. In fact, the Bible tells us that, "the eyes of the Lord run to and from throughout the whole earth, to show Himself strong on behalf of those whose heart is loyal to Him" (2 Chronicles 16:9).

The account of the life of King Hezekiah is recorded in 2 Kings 18—20, 2 Chronicles 29-32 and Isaiah 36-39. The studies that follow will be based on expositions of selected portions from those chapters. In chapter one, we will look at Hezekiah's personal relationship with God. An intimate and dynamic relationship with God is the foundation for any spiritual renewal. Nothing can substitute for relationship with God. We will examine, therefore, how Hezekiah related correctly to God. In doing so he made sure that his walk was right.

In chapter two we will look at how he *restored God's glory* to his nation. We will examine some of the decisive steps he took to accomplish such a task. Spiritual renewal is always marked by a new fervour in worship. In spiritual renewals, vain, ritualistic and mundane worship comes to an end, and, new excitement and zeal infuse worship with passion and glorious praise. *Hezekiah's worship was right.*

In chapter three we will look at how he *rebelled against the enemy* (Assyria). Revival time is, of necessity, warfare time. This is because the Devil will do anything and everything to oppose that which is dedicated to glorifying God. If attention to one's *walk* is important in the quest for revival, and attention to one's *worship* is important in the quest for revival, then attention to one's *warfare* is also important in the quest for revival. As we seek revival there will be more intense battles with the forces of evil. Satan is against deliberate and relentless pursuit for God and His glory. This chapter will identify some of the crucial elements in Hezekiah's preparation for *warfare* that led to his great victory.

In chapter four we will see how Hezekiah *resorted to fervent prayers*. In effect, this chapter can be considered part two of Hezekiah's warfare. Prayer is such an important ingredient in spiritual renewal that it deserves a chapter for itself. It is fervent prayer in passionate pursuit for God that will escort revival.

Chapter five will examine how Hezekiah *responded to the blessings of God*. Revival is accompanied by great blessings, even unprecedented blessings. Therefore, it is important that we anticipate the blessings of God. It is even more important that we consider, and commit ourselves to, an appropriate response to God's intervention. Our responsibility does not end when God sends revival. He watches to see how we respond to the blessings of revival. It is in this area that we find Hezekiah's *weakness*.

As you read these chapters and meditate on the Scripture passages, it is my prayer that God will ignite your heart with revival fire. To this end, let us pray in the words of J. Edwin Orr:

> O Holy Ghost, revival comes from Thee;
> Send a revival- start a work in me.
> Thy word declares Thou wilt supply our need;
> For blessings now, O Lord, I humbly pray.[16]

I

HEZEKIAH'S WALK

He Related Correctly to God

¹ Now it came to pass in the third year of Hoshea the son of Elah, king of Israel, that Hezekiah the son of Ahaz, king of Judah, began to reign. ² He was twenty-five years old when he became king, and he reigned twenty nine-nine years in Jerusalem. His mother's name was Abi the daughter of Zechariah. ³ And he did what was right in the sight of the Lord, according to all that his father David had done. ⁴ He removed the high places and broke the sacred pillars, cut down the wooden image and broke in pieces the bronze serpent that Moses had made; for until those days the children of Israel burned incense to it, and called it Nehushtan. ⁵ He trusted in the Lord God of Israel, so that after him was none like him among all the kings of Judah, nor who were before him. ⁶ For he held fast to the Lord; he did not depart from following Him, but kept his commandments, which the Lord had commanded Moses. ⁷ The Lord was with him; he prospered wherever he went. And he rebelled against the king of Assyria and did not serve him (2 Kings 18:1-7).

The biblical account of Hezekiah's life begins with some interesting statements concerning his relationship with God. One principle we learn from this account is that the quality of service that King Hezekiah gave to God was directly proportionate to the quality of his relationship with God. Generally, the performance of the kings of Judah is evaluated against the life of King David. Hezekiah is one of the few who compared favourably with his forefather David. The other good kings were Asa (1 Kings 5:11), Jehosaphat (2 Kings 22:43) and Josiah (2 Kings 22:2).[17] However, Jehosaphat did not remove the high places.[18] The Bible says of King Hezekiah:

> ...he trusted in the Lord God of Israel, so that after him was none like him among all the kings of Judah, nor who were before him (2 Kings 18:6).

What a commentary the Lord had of Hezekiah! What evaluation would the Lord have of your life? It was the solid relationship that Hezekiah had with the Lord that formed the bedrock of his spiritual impact on his nation.

The foundation of any revival is leadership that enjoys dynamic and personal relationship with God. Yet, many of us tend to miss the point and continue to,

> ...become consumed with the work of God while neglecting our relationship with Him. We get so busy doing the things of God that we sacrifice our walk with God.[19]

Sacrificing relating to God for working for God is fatal for revival preparing. Nothing can substitute for relationship with God. Natural abilities cannot substitute for relationship. Reputation cannot substitute for relationship. Academic qualification cannot substitute for relationship, even if we have more degrees than a thermometer. Popularity cannot substitute for relationship. Sophisticated programmes and avant *garde* technology cannot substitute for relationship. God wants us to be personally acquaint-ed with Him, so that we can commune with him as 'friend with friend.' God longs for this kind of intimacy with the masterpiece of His creation, us.

Tommy Tenny has put it well. He says,

> There is a vast difference between having an encounter with God and having a relationship with Him. It's like the difference between a sprint and a marathon. Anyone can start a marathon-but the honour goes to those who finish and finish well.
> The marathon is more than just a Sunday morning "fun run." It requires dedication, determination, and discipline. It means staying the course—running even when you'd rather give up and collapse. Stamina and direction can be more important than speed.[20]

Developing a solid relationship with the Lord takes deliber-ate actions, of doing and undoing. It cannot be left to chance. Let us examine some of the specific things that the Bible says about Hezekiah that underscore his relationship with God.

A. He did right in the sight of the Lord (verse 3)

Verse three of our text tells us that Hezekiah "did what was right in the sight of the Lord, according to all that his father Da-vid had done." Hezekiah was committed to doing that which was "right." For Hezekiah, what was considered "right" was not deter-mined by what others thought, or said, but what was commanded by God. That which was "right" for Hezekiah was consistent with what was "right" in the sight of the Lord. That which is "right" for us must not be determined by the most contemporary research, or what may be the most viable economic option, or the most popular opinion, or the most convenient situation, or the most comfortable choice. "Right" must be determined by that which the Lord commands.

Many times we can be "right" in the sight of others but be wrong in the sight of the Lord. The converse is also true. Oftentimes we may appear wrong in the eyes of people but we are right in the sight of the Lord. In those times, when we are right in God's sight, we must stand by our conviction, even if we have to take much criticism or flack. We ought to obey God rather than men (Acts 5:29). It was Martin Luther who said, "my conscience is captive to the word of God and it is neither right nor safe to go against one's conscience."[21]

Too often we seek to dismiss the uncomfortable feelings that we experience as the Holy Spirit tugs at our conscience. But such tugs are to make us know that we are doing wrong. The more we resist the dictates of our conscience, the more we will become insensitive to the Spirit, and so fail to discern between good and evil. Many people stifle their conscience until it has become "dead", as if seared with a hot iron (1 Timothy 4:2). May God help us to always seek to do that which is right in the sight of the Lord, for the Bible tells us: "The eyes of the Lord are in every place, Keeping watch on the evil and the good" (Proverbs 15:3). God, who sees and knows all, will chastise us for doing wrong rather than "right."

The word translated "right" in our text (verse three) is the Hebrew word *yasar,* which may also be translated "straight."[22] Hezekiah was committed to doing that which was straight in the eyes of the Lord. Are you committed to being straight in all your dealings? Or, are there crooked ways that you need to straighten immediately?

If God should put His plumb line against you today, how would you measure up? How are you in your dealings with money? How is your relationship with members of the opposite sex? How do you deal with power? What about your dealings with legal documents and taxes? Are your conversations pleasing to the Lord?

God's standard is still perfection. What He told ancient Israel applies to modern Christians. Just as He delivered Israel from Egypt, so has He delivered us from hell. "For I am the Lord who brings you up out of the land of Egypt, to be your God. You shall therefore be holy, for I am holy." In today's world, in which moral standards are being eroded by *relativism,* God still has absolutes. Relativism states that *right* is defined by what is right for you, or right for the particular circumstance. In effect, everything is relative and so there are no absolute standards of right and wrong. However, the sovereign Creator of this universe still has absolute standards of right and wrong. Life is not a free-for-all. We are expected to be straight in the eyes of the Lord.

Leaders especially are called to be straight. The Bible stipulates that leaders should be blameless (1 Timothy 3:2, Titus 1:7). Lack of correct alignment with God becomes more evident with each advance in leadership. No wonder many leaders are haunted by their past when they hit the spotlight. Dr. Neil Anderson says: "if leaders sweep repeated offences under the rug, they will soon trip over them."[23]

If you lead the flock of God you are under divine obligation to walk straight, even as Jesus walked (1 John 2:6). We are called to walk circumspectly (Ephesians 5:15). An airplane travelling one degree off course will never reach its destination. Hezekiah was committed to being straight. He was absolutely straight. He was absolutely upright. If you please, Hezekiah was downright upright.

In a sinful and perverse world, those who are committed to being straight do so at the expense of being considered radical, and even fanatical. However, God's children must remember that they are citizens of another Kingdom, and as such, they must live according to the principles of that Kingdom.

May God grant us the courage to do what is right, for it is not sufficient to know what is right! "Therefore, to him who knows to do good and does not do it, to him it is sin" (James 4:17). May God give us that unswerving commitment to do the right, at all times, and under all circumstances. However, right actions can only flow out of a heart that is right. Stanley Grenz makes this principle clear:

> In the postmodern world we must reappropriate the older pietist discovery that a "right heart" takes primacy over a "right head." Theology must take its lodging in the heart, for it is concerned with the transformation of not only the intellectual commitments, but also the character of the life of the believer.[24]

Intellect and morality must go together. Hezekiah showed this. Not only was King Hezekiah committed to doing right but he was also committed to removing idolatry, for our relationship with God calls us not only to do some things, but also to undo other things.

B. He removed idolatry (verse 4)

Hezekiah was committed to an activist faith. He believed in doing things for God, in putting his faith into action. We read how he

...removed the high places and broke the sacred pillars, cut down the wooden image and broke in pieces the bronze serpent that Moses had made; for until those days the children of Israel burned incense to it and called it Nehushtan (2Kings 18:4).

Hezekiah realized that if he were going to have a dynamic relationship with the Almighty God he had to remove idolatry. Judah had denigrated to become an idolatrous nation. The people were sucked into the Canaanite worship that prevailed around them. They disregarded the very clear injunction the Lord had given to them to observe, when they entered the Promised Land:

You shall not go after other gods, the gods of the peoples who are all around you (for the Lord your God is a jealous God among you), lest the anger of the Lord your God be aroused against you and destroy you from the face of the earth (Deuteronomy 6:14-15).

Regrettably, when Israel entered the Promised Land, they eventually forgot His holy demands. Their negligence invoked

God's wrath. Therefore, Hezekiah deliberately set out to destroy all the altars, which were dedicated to the false gods. He even destroyed the altars upon which mixed worship was being offered. It is grossly offensive to the holy God to equate Him with other gods. The Lord Jehovah is a jealous God and He will not share His glory with anyone, under any circumstance (Exodus 20:5; Deuteronomy 5:9, 6:15). Again, this cuts against the grain of the dominant postmodern philosophy of religious truth, called religious pluralism. Ajith Fernando states:

> Religious pluralism says that there is no such thing as absolute truth. Therefore the different religions are "equals in the universe of faiths," as John Hick, the foremost pluralist in the church said.[25]

Under false notions of tolerance, then, religious pluralism develops and leads to religious syncretism. Therefore, the challenge that the nation of Judah faced during the time of Hezekiah is similar to the challenge that we now face in our post-modern era, that is, the challenge of religious pluralism that leads to religious syncretism. Religious syncretism refers to the practice of mixing Christianity with other religions. But in God's economy, no religion is compatible with Christianity, defined in terms of genuine worship to the One, True, Living God. Again, Fernando has this to say of syncretism:

> Syncretism takes place when, in an effort to identify with non-Christians, elements essential to the gospel are dropped or elements incompatible with the gospel are taken on in the practice and presentation of Christianity.[26]

Christianity is unique and exclusive. The Christian faith must not be mixed with any other. Many times the problem is not that God's people have completely turned away from Him, but that they have tried to worship Him alongside other gods. That will never work. He must be Lord of all or not at all. He will not accept mixed worship. The Apostle Paul warns us that we cannot drink simultaneously at the Lord's Table and at the Devil's table (1 Corinthians 10:21). Some of those who tried that were afflicted with unnecessary suffering and some did die prematurely (1 Corinthians 11:30). Jesus emphatically states:

> No one can serve two masters; for either he will hate the one and love the other, or else he will be loyal to the one and despise the other. You cannot serve God and mammon" (Matthew 6:24).

True worship of the God of the Bible must be decisive. That's why the prophet Elijah had to confront his nation with the words: "How long will you falter between two opinions? If the Lord is God, follow Him; but if Baal, follow him" (1 Kings 21). The Lord will not accept contaminated worship. He will spew it out of His mouth. He requires total allegiance. He is seeking for true worshippers who will worship Him in spirit and in truth (John 4:24)

If you desire to have a dynamic relationship with God, you must remove idolatry from your life. Anything that takes the place of God in your life is an idol. Mark Bubeck says, "idolatry takes place when we physically or mentally put anything before God."[27] You don't necessarily have to worship a god of wood or stone to be an idolater.

Your job can become your god. Your possessions can become your god. Someone can become your god. Even your belly can become your god (Romans 16:18). Rick Richardson has pointed out that gods have a spiritual reality that rules our lives, whether they are material, physical, relational or occult.[28]

Rick Richardson further asserts that they may become personal and societal demons that rule our lives. For example, "in the case of sex and alcohol, they can become powerful addictions, exerting their rule in our lives in horrifying and destructive ways."[29]

The power of those false gods must not be underestimated. That is why we must ask God to "break down every idol" so that we may worship Him in spirit and in truth, and not be controlled by idolatry. The scripture calls us to lay aside every weight and every besetting sin so that we can run the race that is set before us (Hebrews 12:1). If our relationship is going to be more than mediocre, we have got to, consciously and deliberately, lay aside every hindrance. Tommy Tenny has pointed out that this job of "unloading" is not God's, but ours.[30]

Our responsibility then is to seek out and root out all false gods, for even good things can become idols. The passage tells us that Hezekiah destroyed the Serpent that Moses had made (Numbers 21). Even things that God used in the past may become idols. Things that we have inherited in our culture may be idolatrous. Church traditions can become idols. Therefore, we must continually face the challenge of making the gospel relevant to our time and contexts, lest we occupy ourselves with defending rituals that are meaningless. Hezekiah found it necessary, not surprisingly, to re-examine his heritage.

C. He re-examined his heritage (verse 4)

One of the things that Hezekiah inherited in his time was the Serpent Moses had used miraculously. God had directed Moses to make a brazen Serpent while the Children of Israel were travelling through the wilderness. This Serpent was lifted up on a pole so that when snakes bit people they could look at it, and recover. Those who looked up at the Serpent on the pole were instantly healed (Numbers 21). God used the symbol of the uplifted Serpent mightily in the wilderness. It was God's provision for healing and deliverance for those who were poisoned by the venom of the snake.

The uplifted Serpent, a foreshadowing of the uplifted Christ, was a symbol of life and hope. It was an instrument of healing and deliverance. There is no doubt that the elevated brazen serpent was used powerfully by God to accomplish His purposes. However, with the passing of time, the brazen serpent had lost its significance. It became associated with Canaanite serpent worship. Therefore, when Hezekiah came to the throne, he recognized that the brazen serpent was no longer glorifying to God. In fact, it had become idolatrous. Therefore, Hezekiah had no option but to destroy it.

We learn from this that there may be once precious things that we now need to remove from our lives and ministry as we reaffirm Christian spirituality in the emerging post-modern era. In the book *The Challenge of Postmodernism: An Evangelical Engagement* David Dockery made this point:

> As we move into the twenty-first century, a new way of viewing the world has emerged. The "modern" way of thinking, that dominated the nineteenth and twentieth cen-

turies have become obsolete. These modern ideas no longer seem relevant. The twenty-first century will be characterized as the "postmodern age." This postmodern world becomes the new challenge of the evangelical church.[31]

Dockery's observations are relevant. Things that God used mightily in the past may become idolatrous in later generations, not because they have become sinful in themselves, but because they have become irrelevant. The emergence of post-modernism will certainly render some of our methods and paradigms obsolete. Even in the church strategies and practices may become obsolete.

Like the children of Issachar, who had "understanding of the times" to know what Israel ought to do, we too must understand the times in which we live and minister appropriately (1 Chronicles 12:32). We have a responsibility to apply the gospel of Jesus relevantly and meaningfully to the generation in which we live. David, the Bible tells us, served the Lord well in his generation. To fulfil this responsibility we cannot be indifferent to the realities of the time in which we minister. We are currently travailing in the mega-change from modernism to post-modernism. Therefore, we have to know why we are doing what we are doing.

In his book, *Strategic Planning: A New Model for Church and Ministry Leaders*, Aubrey Malphurs makes this valuable observation:

> Every institution—whether for profit or not for profit-must wrestle with the vexing question of what in the organization should change and what should never change. Opinions in both contexts range from one extreme (nothing should change) to the other (everything should change). Thus it

is imperative that the church and its leaders have a biblical theology of change that guides them, especially during the pounding when it is difficult to think. A good theology of change addresses two areas: function and form.[32]

The "functions" of the church refer to those timeless truths that must never change. Examples of these functions are evangelism, worship, prayer and fellowship. These are "constants" for the church, whether of the first century or the 21st century. On the other hand, the "forms" of the church are "timely vehicles which are tied in some way to the church's culture."[33] For example, some of the "forms" of the church are hymns, open-air meetings, cell groups, evangelistic campaigns, and gospel films. These may change with time, for as new and more effective methods emerge, we may employ them to accomplish the purpose of the church, that of making disciples of Jesus Christ (Matthew 28:16-20).

In carrying out this Great Commission, every generation is under divine obligation to subject its culture to scriptural scrutiny, to guard against practices that might be culturally acceptable but idolatrous. Every culture will have traditions and practices inherited from past generations that need such scrutiny. These practices must be evaluated in the light of the Word of God. This is because the meaning of traditions may change with time. Traditional practices may lose original significance and take on new meaning. Methodologies that have been on the cutting edge in the past may become dull in contemporary evangelism.

In their book *Church Next*, Eddie Gibbs and Ian Cofey state:

> ...while the gospel supports some cultural affirmations and fulfils some unrealised cultural aspirations, it also

addresses the demonic element present in every culture. Therefore, contextualization is from a critical, not naïve standpoint [34]

There is much talk today about contextualization. But what is contextualization? Contextualization "takes place when the presentation and outworking of the gospel are done in a way that fits the context."[35] Contextualization is a strategy that emerges as we engage in the struggle to make the gospel relevant to our sociological contexts. Contextualization is what we must always do. We must continually subject our traditions to scriptural scrutiny.

Of course, it is not only church traditions that must be subjected to scriptural scrutiny for validity. Cultural practices, in general, which have been inherited, must be evaluated too, in light of the Word of God. This is particularly relevant to Caribbean believers, for much of Caribbean culture is a mixture of Christianity and pagan cultural retentions, from Africa, India, Europe, and China.

Yet, we must not unduly reject our rich cultural expressions for imported ones. When the Word of God is applied to the core of our culture it establishes genuine roots. And when such happens, Christianity does not become a superficial coating on the culture. As the Caribbean church matures there is a place for what is now referred to as, 'Caribbean Theology,' defined by Jamaican theologian Ashley Smith as, "an attempt by Caribbean Christians to interpret the revelations of God within their particular historical, ethic, political, and cultural context."[36] The key in all of this is to affirm both biblical authenticity and cultural relevance.

If we are going to have a dynamic relationship with the Lord, then we must subject our heritage to serious scrutiny in light of the revealed Word of God so that we might not unwittingly endorse or embrace ethically questionable or demonic practices. We must not be caught up with anything contrary to the Word of God. We must understand the roots of the rituals we practice, so that we can approve or disapprove them justifiably. We cannot afford to occupy our time just carrying out motions: "having a form of godliness but denying its powers" (2 Timothy 3:5).

The time is too short to try to harvest with a blade that is blunt, or a tool that has completely lost its cutting edge. May we seek God to show us how best we can communicate the gospel of Jesus Christ with all its power, and yet with cultural sensitivity. We must struggle to achieve the correct perspective, for we must neither compromise cultural relevance nor biblical authenticity. Without cultural relevance we apply remedy where people are not hurting, and without biblical authenticity, we apply the wrong antidote altogether. Hezekiah did a great job of re-examining his heritage and discarding what God had rejected. But, that was not all. The secret of his success was that he relied on God.

D. He relied on God (verse 5)

Another important element in the text that tells us about the relationship that Hezekiah had with God is found in verse four: "he trusted in the Lord God of Israel, so that after him was none like him among all the kings of Judah, nor who were before him." That which sets Hezekiah apart from all the kings of Judah is his profound and unwavering trust in the Living God.

When we recall the context in which Hezekiah reigned, and served God, it helps us to understand his level of trust in God. King Hezekiah came to the throne when Assyria, the then super power, was gobbling up the smaller nations in the Fertile Crescent. Hezekiah's father had established a friendship or vassalage between Assyria and Judah. This meant that Judah recognized Assyria as 'the one who calls the shots.' Under King Ahaz's leadership Judah submitted to the dictates of Assyria, and it also paid an annual tribute to Assyria.

However, Hezekiah severed that relationship and stopped paying the annual tribute to Assyria. He decided, instead, to trust in the Living God. He stopped depending on Assyria for security. That clean break with Assyria was necessary for him to serve God wholeheartedly, because if he had continued to serve Assyria, he would have had to give at least formal allegiance to the gods of Assyria. He was not prepared to stoop to such compromise. He was not about to tolerate the worship of other gods. He remembered the commandment well:

> You shall not make for yourselves a carved image-any like-
> ness of anything that is in the heaven above, or that is in the
> earth beneath or that is in the water under the earth; you
> shall not bow down to them nor serve them. For I the Lord
> your God am a jealous God (Exodus 20:4-5).

Hezekiah was willing to trust God, even under life-threatening circumstances. When he had nothing else to hold on to, he still held on to the Word of God.

To break the relationship with Assyria at that time in history was a very bold step. It did not seem logical. It might have appeared to some as religious fanaticism, or outright stupidity, since he deliberately rejected the most natural way for survival. How then did he expect to survive? "He trusted in the Lord God of Israel" (2 Chronicles 18:5). And, he did so even when the wrath of Assyria was turned against Judah.

Hezekiah did not have the military might of David and Solomon. He did not have many horses and chariots. He did not have any alliance with other nations to come to his rescue. But he had God. And he was willing to trust Him. John Knox is credited with the saying: 'One man plus God is a majority.' Hezekiah was confident about being that kind of majority so he acted with authority. He was prepared to stand by his conviction and trust God.

Faith and sight are mutually exclusive. When we are operating in faith we often do not have the support of the natural indicators. That is why those who launch out in faith do well to follow the example of people like Moses, who saw the invisible:

> 24 By faith Moses, when he became of age, refused to be called the son of Pharaoh's daughter, 25 choosing rather to suffer affliction with the people of God than to enjoy the passing pleasures of sin, 26 esteeming the reproach of Christ greater riches than the treasures in Egypt; for he

looked to the reward.27 By faith he forsook Egypt, not fearing the wrath of the king; for he endured as seeing Him who is invisible (Hebrews 11:24-27).

The example of Moses as he exercised faith in God should inspire us, as we seek to do the work of God. Moses had faith in God and His infallible Word. We too must place our faith in God. We have no option, for, "without faith it is impossible to please Him" (Hebrews 11:6). With God all thing are possible (Mark 10:27). That which is impossible for man is possible with God (Matthew 19:26).

The Bible clearly records that Jesus did not do any mighty work in Nazareth because of the people's unbelief (Mark: 6:6). Unbelief is one of the greatest killers of the work of God. The sin of unbelief even brings the very character of God into question.

Unbelief, the opposite of faith, kept the Children of Israel out of the Promised Land for forty years. Unbelief will also keep you out of your spiritual possessions. The Children of Israel, when the forty years had expired, still had to exercise faith to enter the Promised Land. When again it was time to enter they had to cross the Jordan, which was in spate, and the Lord told them to march into the water and it would part.

They did so and as the feet of the priests who carried the Ark of the Covenant touched the water, it parted. The people were then able to cross over on dry ground (Joshua 3). Their entry into the Promised Land was through the gate of faith. They could not get in any other way. We too need to exercise faith in God and step into the water, and see it part. Has God given you a vision that you need to pursue in His name? And are you still waiting? Now may be the time to launch out into the deep for God.

It was the great missionary statesman, William Carey, who once said, "Expect great things from God; attempt great things for God"[37] William Carey as a child was sickly and not well educated. He was born to poor parents in what was described as a "forgotten village in the dullest period of the dullest of all centuries"[38] He was born in the obscure village of Paulerspury, north of London, in 1761. He was working as an apprentice cobbler when the Lord called him to the work of missions. At that time global missions was largely dormant, and so he encountered much opposition and discouragement, even from within the church. Yet, his faith in God led him to accomplish great exploits for God. He became a pioneer missionary to India and today he is regarded as the 'Father of Modern Missions.' One report says this of William Carey:

> William Carey did go to India. He never took a furlough and never returned to England. He stayed for forty-one years, dying there at age seventy-three. When all was said and done, he had translated the complete Bible into six languages, and portions of the Bible into twenty-nine others. He had founded over one hundred schools for the people of India. He had founded Serampore College, which is still training ministers to this day.[39]

It is when we step out in faith into the flood, or the fire, of the unknown future, in response to the call of God, that we experience the miraculous power of God. The candidates that God will use mightily in the world are those who will run the risk of appearing foolish in the eyes of their contemporaries. God will always recognize and reward the courage of those who rise up and act in faith and obedience to divine direction.

God is still trustworthy. You can rely on Him. "Those who trust in the Lord, are like Mount Zion, which cannot be moved, but abides forever" (Psalm 125:1). It always pays to trust in the Living God. David Lloyd George is noted to have made the following profound statements about faith:

- Faith sees the invisible, believes the incredible, and receives the impossible.
- You can't cross a chasm in two small jumps
- Faith, like muscle, grows strong and supple with exercise.

Faith is the key to a successful revival. Hezekiah used that key to bring about revival: "He trusted in the Lord God of Israel, so that after him was none like him among all the kings of Judah, nor who were before him" (2 Kings 18:5).

Launch out now in faith and give God a chance to do that which will not be done otherwise. If you want to see God do great things in your life you just have to trust Him, even if doing so makes you feel vulnerable, or seem foolish. If Peter had waited for consensus from the other disciples in the boat it is hardly likely that he would have walked on water (Matthew 14:29). Sometimes the step of faith has to be taken without popular support. Once you have heard the voice of God, step out in faith. God will not let you down. When God gives the commission He makes the provision. Blackaby and King have made these significant observations:

The kinds of assignments God gives in the Bible are always God-sized. They are always beyond what people can do because He wants to demonstrate His nature, His strength, His provision and His kindness to His people and to a watching world. That is the only way the world will come to know Him.[40]

Few people have entered the realm of faith that makes them trust God for big things. Only a few, therefore, have ever known what it is to experience God at the mountaintop, where the air is clean, unpolluted and invigorating. Blackaby and King further state:

When God lets you know what He wants to do through you, it will be something only God can do. If you have faith in God who called you, you will obey Him and He will bring to pass what He has purposed to do. If you lack faith you will not do what He wants.[41]

And when by faith we discover what God wants us to do, we must let God accomplish it through us. We must simply do what He wills. We must follow Him resolutely, as Hezekiah did.

E. He resolutely followed the Lord (verse 6)

The Bible says that Hezekiah "held fast to the Lord, and did not depart from following him, but kept His commandments which the Lord had commanded Moses" (2 Chronicles 18:6) The word translated "held fast" here in the New King James Version, and which the King James Version translates "clave," is the Hebrew word *dabaq*, which means "to stick as glue."[42] It is the same word that is used in Genesis that says: "therefore a man shall leave his father and mother and be joined (cleave KJV) to his wife, and they both shall become one flesh" (Genesis 2:24) Our relationship with the Lord should be one that can be appropriately described as cleaving to Him, or sticking to Him like glue.

That sticking should be true of our commitment to God, even when circumstances change. Like the marriage vows, that sticking should be "for richer, for poorer, in sickness and in health." It should hold together in the midst of life or in the face of death. The great difference between our commitment to the Lord and the marriage vows is that not even death can sever our relationship from the Lord. In fact, life gets better when a person departs this life to be ushered into the glorious presence of the Lord. Absolutely nothing can separate us from the love of God (Romans 8:35-38). Therefore, let us cling to the Lord unreservedly, for "the suffering of this present time are not worthy to be compared with the glory which shall be revealed in us" (Romans 8:18).

Too many of us give up too easily in the face of the simplest trial or testing. Are you cleaving to the Lord through thick and thin? Or have you given up the struggle? Are you holding on faithfully, even when you do not understand all that is happening in your life? Keep holding on for it is true: 'the hotter the battle, the sweeter the victory'.

The Bible also says of Hezekiah: "he did not depart from following the Lord" (verse 6). Have you somehow departed from following the Lord? In other words, are you now in a backslidden condition, similar to the condition that the nation of Judah was in during the reign of King Hezekiah? Or, have you left your first love like the Ephesian church of Revelation chapter two? Where are you now spiritually? Have you fallen into mediocrity and permissiveness? There is hope!

God in His love and mercy is now calling you to repentance. The admonition from the Lord is: "Remember therefore from where you have fallen; repent and do the first works or else I will come to you quickly and remove your lampstand from its place— unless, you repent" (Revelation 2:5).

Again, the Bible says that Hezekiah "kept" God's commandments. There is no substitute for obedience to the Lord's commands. Jesus states emphatically that if we love Him we must keep His commandments. When Peter affirmed His love for Christ he was told to feed His sheep. Our love for Christ must be translated into action for "to obey is better than sacrifice/ And to heed than the fat of rams" (1 Samuel 15:22).

May God give us the grace to pursue a dynamic relationship with Him, one that that will be the foundation for revival. A casual relationship with God will never bring about revival. It is revival time. Let us pray in the words of Johnson Oatman Jr.:

> Lord, lift me up and let me stand
> By faith on heaven's table land;
> A higher plane than I have found-
> Lord, plant my feet on higher ground.[43]

II

HEZEKIAH'S WORSHIP

He Restored God's Glory to Judah

¹ Hezekiah became king when he was twenty-five years old, and he reigned twenty-nine years in Jerusalem. His mother's name was Abijah the daughter of Zechariah. ²And he did what was right in the sight of the Lord, according to all that his father David had done. ³ In the first year of his reign, in the first month, he opened the doors of the house of the Lord and repaired them. ⁴ Then he brought in the priests and the Levites, and gathered them in the East Square, ⁵ and said to them: "Hear me Levites! Now sanctify yourselves, sanctify the house of the Lord God of your fathers, and carry out the rubbish from the holy place. ⁶ For our fathers have trespassed and done evil in the eyes of the Lord our God; they have forsaken Him, have turned their faces away from the dwelling place of the Lord, and turned their backs on Him. ⁷ They have also shut up the door of the vestibule, put out the lamps, and have not burned incense or offered burnt offerings in the holy place of the God of Israel. ⁸ Therefore the wrath of the Lord fell upon Judah and Jerusalem, and He has given them up to trouble, to desolation, and to jeering, as you see with your eyes. ⁹ For indeed be-

cause of this our fathers have fallen by the sword; and our sons, our daughters and our wives are in captivity. [10] "Now it is in my heart to make a covenant with the Lord God of Israel, that His fierce wrath may turn away from us. [11] My sons, do not be negligent now, for the Lord has chosen you to stand before Him, to serve Him, and that you should minister to him and burn incense" (2 Chronicles 29:1-11).

Having looked at how Hezekiah related correctly to God we will now proceed to look at how he restored God's glory to Judah. We can see from the passage quoted that one of the first things that Hezekiah did when he came to the throne was to focus on worship in his nation. Verse three of the text tells us that, "in the first year of his reign, in the first month, he opened the doors of the house of the Lord and repaired them." He gave priority to the house of the Lord.

The temple was the place where God's presence was entertained. It was the place where people met with God and offered sacrifices to Him. However, that temple had become neglected and rejected. Worship was put on the back burner. Therefore, when he came to the throne, Hezekiah sought to put back worship in its proper place, as a matter of priority.

A. W. Towzer once said, "Worship is the missing jewel of the evangelical church."[44] Without a proper foundation in worship all else that we do for God becomes superficial and mechanical. In the Evangelical Training Association book entitled Growing Toward Spiritual Maturity, the authors make the very profound statement, "Divorced from true worship, evangelism can become merely a program attached to an already overloaded ecclesiastical machine."[45]

God wants His presence to be among His people. He wants to commune intimately with the masterpiece of His creation, human beings. We were created with the capacity to worship God. Worship is not an elective. It is a part of our core curriculum. It must be our primary occupation, and even supreme preoccupation. If worship of the Living God does not occupy a central place in our lives, then worship of someone else, or something else, will occupy that place for human beings have an innate desire to worship. It is God's plan for human beings to worship Him, and worship Him in spirit and in truth. God is on a search for such true worshippers (John 4:23).

However, many times we get so caught up with ministering to other people that we forget that our primary ministry is to the Lord. In other words, our work for God often undermines our worship of God. We were created primarily to worship God. When time ends and earth is no more God's people will be worshipping Him perpetually. Why then do we do so little of it now? Perhaps we do not give God the quality worship that we should because we do not know God enough. In his book *Apostolic Foundations: The Challenge of Living an Authentic Christian Life* Arthur Katz says:

> If we are going to be a vital church in word, deed and presence and one that is going to fulfil the eternal purposes of God, then something critical is required, namely, **the knowledge of the reality of God.** This is the only thing that will save us from being mere technicians."[46]

God is not looking for worshippers who are "mere technicians." He is looking for true worshippers. From the dawn of creation to the consummation of time and into eternity, it is God's plan to share intimately with His children.

In the book of Genesis, God came down in the cool of the day in the Garden of Eden and communed with Adam. Sin broke that intimate relationship, but praise be to God, we can be reconciled to God through the precious blood of Jesus Christ. God paid the ultimate price to restore human beings to an intimate relationship with Him in Jesus Christ. The essence of the gospel is that Jesus died and arose from the dead to bridge the gap between divinity and humanity.

When God was leading the children of Israel through the wilderness He commanded Moses to make a tabernacle to entertain His presence. He told Moses to make the tabernacle exactly like the pattern shown him on the Mount. God is very particular about the kind of setting in which He will manifest His presence. He will not manifest His presence in places where there is outright disobedience to His will and purposes.

Moses made the tabernacle as directed by the Lord, and the Children of Israel travelled with it in the wilderness. Periodically, they would pitch the tabernacle so that anyone who sought the Lord could enter His presence. Here is one account of Moses entering the tabernacle, and the significant impact that such had on the people:

> 7 Moses took his tent and pitched it outside the camp, far from the camp, and called it the tabernacle of meeting. And it came to pass *that* everyone who sought the Lord went out to the tabernacle of meeting which *was* outside the camp. 8 So it was, whenever Moses went out to the tabernacle, *that* all the people rose, and each man stood *at* his tent door and watched Moses until he had gone into the tabernacle. 9 And it came to pass, when Moses entered the

tabernacle, that the pillar of cloud descended and stood *at* the door of the tabernacle, and *the Lord* talked with Moses. *10* All the people saw the pillar of cloud standing *at* the tabernacle door, and all the people rose and worshiped, each man *in* his tent door. *11* So the Lord spoke to Moses face to face, as a man speaks to his friend. And he would return to the camp, but his servant Joshua the son of Nun, a young man, did not depart from the tabernacle (Exodus 33:7-1).

When Israel became established as a monarchy, a permanent structure was built to entertain the presence of the Lord. This temple was built and dedicated to God by King Solomon. It was a magnificent structure. Here is an excerpt of the account of the dedication of this temple:

> …it came to pass, when the priests came out of the holy place, that the cloud filled the house of the Lord, so that the priests could not continue ministering because of the cloud: for the glory of the Lord filled the house of the Lord (1 Kings 8:10-11).

The presence of the Holy God saturated the atmosphere in the temple. However, 200 years later, during the reign of King Hezekiah, the same temple was dilapidated, dirty and neglected. Indeed, the glory had departed. It was Hezekiah's passion to restore God's glory to His house, and to the nation of Judah. May God give us that same passion to see the earth filled with the knowledge of the glory of the Lord, as the waters cover the sea (Habakkuk 1:14). Hezekiah recognised that it was important to have the glorious presence of God with him if he were going to lead his people in God's direction. He recognized, therefore, that it was not only important for his walk to be right but also that his worship be right. He not only related correctly to God but he restored true worship to Judah. Worship was a matter of priority for him.

Now, while it is true that God knows everything (omniscient) and is everywhere at the same time (omnipresent), it is also true that God is enthroned in the praises of His people (Psalm 22:3). There are times when God chooses to intensify His presence in particular places and times, but first the stage must be set. Indeed, when the stage is set God will perform. And, it always makes a difference when God's presence is displayed within the human environment. People are desperately longing to see God at work in our time. People are not impressed any more with mere human knowledge and skill. They need something more. Blackaby and King have said:

> If people in your community are not responding to the gospel like you see in the New Testament, one possible reason is that they are not seeing God in what you are doing as a church. [47]

The contemporary mindset has recognized the bankruptcy of scientific empiricism and philosophic rationalism, which were the hallmark of the modern era (also referred to as the Enlightenment era). Those standards were hailed as the ultimate grounds for truth. Empiricists postulate that truth is obtained through the examination of testable data. Rationalists, on the other hand, emphasize the role and rule of logic and reason. Therefore, truth had to be testable, logical and reasonable.

So, during the modern period there was little or no place for knowledge that was not scientifically testable, logical or rational. The world was largely seen as a closed system and there was hardly any place for the spiritual. This sophisticated modern period reigned from 1789 to 1989, that is, from the French Revolution to the collapse of Communism.[48]

However, since 1989, the world has been experiencing a shift from modernity to post-modernity. In this period of post modernity, there is a growing quest for supernatural power and spirituality. People are now looking for experience even before explanation.[49] Post modernity is marked by openness to supernatural power and spirituality. The danger is that if this third millennium generation cannot find satisfaction to their searching for spirituality and power in Christian worship, they will seek to satisfy their deep yearnings through other expressions of spirituality and power, even in the realms of the demonic.

Postmodernism then is not about dry orthodoxy (right doctrine). Such is not appealing in the post-modern era. The youths of this millennium, now being designated millennialists, are not attracted by sluggish and mundane worship. Doctrines must be accurate, but worship must also be appealing. Fernando has pointed out that worship can provide a wonderful opportunity for evangelism in this post-modern era. Rick Richardson expressed the same view when he said: "Genuine worship is especially helpful in evangelism today because it can be an authentic experience of the reality of God in community."[50] With reference to the place of worship evangelism he puts it even more pointedly:

> Worship evangelism may be the most significant means of evangelism in the next century, because it combines authenticity and vulnerability with a genuine experience of God's presence. [51]

Therefore, we must do all we can to demonstrate the kingdom, power and glory of God in our generation. And, there is nothing that sets the stage for this like dynamic worship.

Yes, it is God's desire to manifest His glorious presence and love among us, but He is waiting for us to lay out the red carpet for Him to make His grand entry. O that God's people would cry out like Moses of old, "Show me your glory" (Exodus 33:16). May we not be contented to see the grace and the goodness of the Lord only but to see too His glory manifested among us. Let us not only seek the favours of God but as well the face of God.[52] Tommy Tenny has said, "His favour flows where His face is directed."[53] When the Lord says, "Seek My face," we must answer, "Your face, Lord, will I seek" (Psalm 27:8).

Moses recognized that without God's intimate presence he would be doomed to failure, and so he cried to the Lord, "Show me your glory." O how we long to see the earth filled with the knowledge of the glory of the Lord, even as "the waters cover the sea" (Habakkuk 2:14). The Bible tells us that if we draw near to God He will draw near to us (James 4:8). Yes, "the eyes of the Lord run to and fro throughout the whole earth, to show Himself strong on behalf of those whose heart is loyal to Him" (2 Chronicles 16:9).

If we are going to see the presence of the Lord manifested among us, we must deliberately prepare ourselves to entertain Him. Hezekiah made some deliberate steps to entertain the presence of the Lord in Judah, and we can learn some important lessons from examining these steps. The first step that Hezekiah took to restore God's glory to his nation was to repair the temple.

A.   *He Repaired the Temple (Verse 3)*

When Hezekiah came to the throne, the temple of the Lord was in a dilapidated condition. It had been neglected for many years. Temple worship was being marginalized and altars were set up all over Judah. The people no longer found it convenient to gather together in Jerusalem to offer sacrifices unto God. But, Hezekiah saw that it was imperative for God's house to be in order if it were truly going to entertain His glorious presence. In our time, there is often disorder in God's house. Some who make up the house often become out of order. But God requires order in His house. The Word of God makes it clear that God's house must be set in order for God's glory to fill the house.

Could it be that God's glory is not being manifested among us today to the extent that we would like to see it because His temple is being neglected? The Bible tells us that in our time God does not dwell in temples made with hands, for our bodies are the temples of the Holy Ghost. It is therefore our divine obligation to present our bodies a living sacrifice, holy and acceptable unto God for such is our "spiritual act of worship" (Romans 12:1 NIV). No wonder we hear the apostle Paul admonishing us:

> Do you not know that you are the temple of God and that the Spirit of God dwells in you? If anyone defiles the temple of God, God will destroy him. For the temple of God is holy, which temple you are (1 Corinthians 3:16-17).

How many of us have really taken that seriously? Listen again to the Apostle's passionate plea, with detailed explanation added, to press home his admonition:

> Flee sexual immorality. Every sin that a man does is out-
> side the body, but he who commits sexual immorality sins
> against his own body. Or do you not know that your body is
> the temple of the Holy Spirit who is in you, whom you have
> from God, and you are not your own? For you were bought
> at a price; therefore glorify God in your body and in your
> spirit, which are God's (1 Corinthians 6:16-20).

It can be asserted with certainty, then, that the spiritual
temple of the Lord must be repaired if His presence is going to feel
comfortable in it, in revival power.

In February 2002 Jamaica had the privilege of hosting Her
Majesty, Queen Elizabeth the Second, for a few days as part of her
Majesty's Jubilee Celebrations. Our government spent millions of
dollars preparing for the royal visit. The house in which the Queen
was entertained, King's House, was renovated. The carpets and
curtains were changed. And rightly so, for, the presence of digni-
taries must be entertained with respect. Proper protocol must be
exercised to entertain royalty.

At another level, we have the unsurpassed privilege to entertain in our house, the King of kings and Lord of lords, the Creator of heaven and earth. Yet, we often treat His majestic presence
with disdain. There must be awe in the temple, and order, for the
temple is the dwelling place of the Most High God.

Our bodies are the temples of the Holy Spirit. God lives in
us. God does not live in temples made with hands anymore (Acts
7:48; Acts 17:24), but He now dwells in the spiritual temple that is
made up of both Jews and Gentiles who have accepted Jesus Christ
as personal Saviour. It is a tremendous privilege to know that God,
Almighty, has chosen to take up residence in us.

Because God lives in us we must give due regard to His divine presence by keeping our temples clean. Whereas in the Old Testament God's presence was entertained in the tabernacle (built by Moses) and later the Temple (built by Solomon and rebuilt after the exile), in the New Testament God dwells in the midst of His people, His spiritual temple (being built by Jesus Christ). Jesus is still building this temple,

> ...in whom the whole building, being fitted together, grows into a holy temple in the Lord, in whom you also are being built together for a dwelling place of God in the Spirit (Ephesians 2:21-22).

What a glorious privilege to be a part of this glorious temple. It is interesting to note that the physical Jewish temple was destroyed in 70 A. D., and it has never been rebuilt. It was God's intention to dwell in the lives of His people instead of a temple made of wood and stone. May the glory of the risen Christ be manifested in His living temple today. The glorious presence of the Lord was manifested in the tabernacle and in the temple (Exodus 33:9; 2 Chronicles 1:2) in the Old Testament, in magnificent ways. His presence must continue to be manifested through His spiritual temple in our time. May we heed the exhortation of Matthew: "Let your light so shine before men, that they may see your good works and glorify your Father in heaven"(Matthew 5:16)

We must each seek to become then, God's lighted temple. The fact that our bodies are the temples of the Holy Spirit has great implications for what we do with our bodies. Every member of our bodies must be completely yielded to the Holy Spirit. Again, the Scriptures give us very clear warning in this regard:

9 Do you not know that the unrighteous will not inherit the kingdom of God? Do not be deceived. Neither fornicators, nor idolaters, nor adulterers, nor homosexuals, nor sodomites, 10 nor thieves, nor covetous, nor drunkards, nor revilers, nor extortioners will inherit the kingdom of God. 11 And such were some of you. But you were washed, but you were sanctified, but you were justified in the name of the Lord Jesus and by the Spirit of our God...15 Do you not know that your bodies are members of Christ? Shall I then take the members of Christ and make *them* members of a harlot? Certainly not! 16 Or do you not know that he who is joined to a harlot is one body *with her*? For *"the two,"* He says, *"shall become one flesh."* 17 But he who is joined to the Lord is one spirit *with Him*.18 Flee sexual immorality. Every sin that a man does is outside the body, but he who commits sexual immorality sins against his own body. 19 Or do you not know that your body is the temple of the Holy Spirit *who is* in you, whom you have from God, and you are not your own? 20 For you were bought at a price; therefore glorify God in your body and in your spirit, which are God's (1 Corinthians 6:20).

The Apostle presses us to know certain things about God's temple. Do we really know those things? What the apostle says makes it clear that the temple of the Lord must be given attention. Is your spiritual temple in need of repair? It could be that the pleasure of this world, or simply your busy schedule, has caused you to neglect your temple. Your temple may need major repairs, or it may simply need dusting. Whatever the problem is with your temple, the agent to cleanse it is the blood of Jesus Christ. Apply the blood and repair the spiritual temple so that the glory of the Lord can be manifested.

Not only did Hezekiah repair the temple of the Lord but he also re-opened the doors of the temple, which his father Ahaz closed.

B. He re-opened the doors of the temple (verse 3)

It is a great tragedy when the doors of the temple are closed. Hezekiah was determined to open those closed doors so that people could once again come into the presence of the Holy God, so that God's presence could once again come among His people. Have you noticed any door to your temple that is closed? Have you noticed a door closed that was once open to welcome people into the presence of the Lord? Have you recently closed some doors in your own life, doors once open to entertain the awesome presence of God in your life? If so, it is time to re-open those doors and let God come in with new power, or as Jim Cymbala would say, with "fresh wind and fresh fire."

In your church it could be that you have inherited some closed doors, even some doors that have been closed for years, decades, or even centuries. If so, God is perhaps impressing it upon your heart to reopen those doors. It doesn't matter that you didn't close them. God may still call you to reopen them. Hezekiah re-opened the doors that his father Ahaz had closed.

God may very well call us to undo what some of our predecessors have done wrong. He may also call us to restart some of the things that they did right and that we are not now doing. All persons have divine obligations to minister faithfully in their generation, like David, for we are in God's kingdom for such a time as this.

It is time to reopen the closed doors so that God can come and fill His temple; closed doors of extended prayer meetings, closed doors of fasting, closed doors of diligent Bible Study, closed doors of scripture memorization, closed doors of witnessing, to mention a few. It is a sad reality when we hear the Lord saying to the Church of Laodicea:

> Behold, I stand at the door and knock. If anyone hears my voice and opens the door, I will come in to him and dine with him, and he with Me (Revelation 3:20).

Notice in that Scripture God's individual appeal. Will you let Him in? The songwriter presses home the same point. He says:

> Time after time He has waited before,
> And now He is waiting again
> To see if you're willing to open the door-
> O how He wants to come in.[54]

O how God wants to come in and fill the temple with the glory of His majestic presence! It is a tragedy when temple doors are closed. People who need to come in are locked out. God Himself is locked out. Prayerfully ask the Lord, right now, to show you any closed door in your life or ministry that needs to be reopened so that the glory of His presence may fill His temple.

C. He reinstated the priests and the Levites (verse 4)

Another decisive step that Hezekiah took in restoring God's glory to his nation was to reinstate the priests and the Levites. The priests and the Levites were specially chosen by God to give attention to His work. They were separated unto God and His work. Hezekiah realised that if the work of God were going to be accomplished in all its fullness then all the priests and Levites would have to be in their proper places.

But, the reality at the time was that all the priests and Levites had long left the service of God. They were otherwise occupied. Nothing of significance can happen when those whom God has appointed and anointed turn away from their divine calling. The priests and the Levites are needed to minister before the Lord. Ministry to the Lord must take priority over ministry to men and women. Arthur Katz says:

> ...we have fallen so far from the sense of priestliness that we consider service to men to be the highest expression we can or need to attain. We regard the sweat of our exertion in **that** service as evidence of our approval, but **God** sees it otherwise. The heavenly priest comes out from the holiest place, out from waiting upon God, out from being emptied from his own good ideas, good intentions and methods. He lets go of his own order of service, his own message, his own selection of songs, and comes forth with that which is given by **God.** We need to see more such people who are willing to forsake their own intentions.[55]

We need to have then, a strong sense of our priestly responsibility as we represent our fellowmen before God and come to our fellowmen on behalf of God. If we are going to experience true revival we must be faithful to this dual divine calling. Under the new covenant every believer is a priest unto God.

> But you are a chosen generation, a royal priesthood, a holy nation, His own special people, that you may proclaim the praises of Him who has called you out of darkness into His marvellous light (1 Peter 2:9).

The Bible makes clear our priestly responsibility. God calls us to minister unto God and then to minister unto humanity. Again, Arthur Katz has emphasized this very well. He says:

> We need more invasions from heaven and such priests who will come and minister before men only after they had first ministered to God in the holy place. We need priestly ministry, ministry from men who have first made sacrifice for themselves, who have first offered up their flesh, their own ambitions, their own vanity, and self deceit, their own fear and greed and man-pleasing.[56]

Such men are needed to lead God's army into revival. They are servants focussed on God and His work, and not on self. Interestingly, the first missionary journey of the church of the Lord Jesus Christ was birthed in the context of ministry to the Lord. Acts 13:2 says:

> as they ministered to the Lord and fasted, the Holy Spirit said, "Now separate to Me Barnabas and Saul for the work to which I have called them."

I believe that in our time, if we become more active in ministering to the Lord we will hear the voice of the Holy Spirit clearer. When we are more into God He will be more into us. For example, if we worship God more we will witness for God more. Experience shows that work for God flows out of worship of God. If work precedes worship the result is worries. Before the priests could be used in the work of the Lord, they had to sanctify themselves, thus making themselves useable in service to God.

D. He removed the filthiness from the holy place (verse 5)

Another decisive step that Hezekiah took to restore true worship to his nation and stem the spiritual bankruptcy was to remove the filthiness, or rubbish, from the holy place. Hezekiah said to the Levites:

> Hear me Levites! Now sanctify yourselves, sanctify the house of the Lord God of your fathers, and carry out the rubbish (filthiness KJV) from the holy place...." (2 Chronicles 29:5)

Filthiness has no place in God's house. Filthiness is sinfulness. The greatest hindrance to revival is sin in the holy place. Sin in the body of Christ is like a malignant cancer in the human body. If it is not removed, and removed quickly, the whole body will become contaminated, and most likely perish. Sin destroys.

Therefore, the child of God must not harbour sin in the holy temple for sin will bring a reproach not only to himself or herself, but to the entire family, church and even the nation at large. No wonder the word of the Lord tells us:

> If My people who are called by My name will humble themselves, and pray and seek my face, and turn from their

wicked ways, then I will hear from heaven, and will forgive
their sin and heal their land (Chronicles 7:14).

The practice of sin in the holy place courts defeat and dis-
grace. God's standard remains high, even in this post-modern age
of relativism. Post-modern relativism teaches that there is no absolute, and so people are free to do whatever pleases them. Right is
defined as whatever works.

However, God is an unchanging God and His standards have
not changed. He is the "same yesterday, today and forever" (Hebrews 13:8). He is still the holy God and He still expects holiness
from His people. Therefore, sin must be removed from His temple,
and removed fast, before judgment falls, for God is a consuming fire
(Hebrews 12:29) and it is a fearful thing to fall into the hands of the
Living God (Hebrews 10:31). The Israelites lost the battle at Ai because one man had disobeyed the command of the Lord (Joshua 7).

The inhabitants of Judah could not advance because of sin. If
they wanted to see the presence and power of the Lord manifested
in their nation, as in former days, they just had to purify the temple
of the Lord. Therefore, they set out to cleanse the temple at the
king's command. The Bible tells us in verses sixteen to nineteen
that after the priest had sanctified themselves they,

> 16 Went into the inner part of the house of the Lord to
> cleanse it, and brought out all the debris that they found
> in the temple of the Lord to the court of the house of the
> Lord. And the Levites took it out and carried it to the
> brook Kidron. 17 Now they began to sanctify on the first
> day of the first month, and on the eighth day of the month
> they came to the vestibule of the Lord. So they sanctified

the house of the Lord in eight days, and on the sixteenth day of the first month they finished.

Notice how detailed was the cleaning of the priests. They took as long as was necessary, even from the first day of the month to the eighth. Notice that they went into every place, including the vestibule. Cleaning is not cleaning if half done. Cleaning must be complete:

> 18 Then they went to King Hezekiah and said, "We have cleansed all the house of the Lord, the alter of burnt offerings with all its articles, and the table of the showbread with all it articles. 19 "Moreover all the articles which King Ahaz in his reign had cast aside in his transgression we have prepared and sanctified; and there they are, before the altar of the Lord (2 Chronicles 29:16-19).

Praise the Lord! It was revival time. The temple of the Lord had been sanctified. The priest and Levites went into the temple and removed all the filth. They took it and dumped it in the Kidron brook. Today, we do not have to take the filthiness to the Kidron brook, for there is another place prepared to deal with the filthiness. That place is Calvary! The songwriter William Cowper tells us:

> There is a fountain filled with blood
> Drawn from Immanuel's veins;
> And sinners plunged beneath that flood
> Lose all their guilty stains;
> Lose all their guilty stains;
> Lose all their guilty stains;
> And sinners plunged beneath that flood
> Lose all their guilty stains.[57]

Thank God! If there is filthiness in the holy place, there is provision for its removal. The Bible tells us: "the blood of Jesus Christ His Son cleanses from all unrighteousness" (1 John 1:7). It also says: "If we confess our sins, He is faithful and just to forgive us our sins and to cleanse us from all unrighteousness" (1 John 1:9).

It doesn't matter how long the filthiness has been in the holy place. It doesn't matter what kind of filthiness. It doesn't even matter who put it there. All that matters is that the blood of Jesus Christ is applied and that it is applied urgently. There is a cure for sin. There is no virtue in trying to cover sin, for "he who covers his sins will not prosper, but whoso confesses and forsakes them will have mercy" (Proverbs 28:13).

Sin in the holy place cannot be overcome by perfume. New and sophisticated programmes cannot compensate for holiness. Sin cannot be swept in a corner and be forgotten. The stench of sin will continue to make the atmosphere unbearable to the Holy God.

Sin has to be removed from the holy place. It must be dealt with decisively in the name and blood of Jesus Christ. God is longing to manifest His presence. He wants to reveal Himself and His plans. He wants the glory of His presence to fill His temple. But He has a major problem if the temple is not sanctified. God wants to do a mighty work in this world but He cannot, until the sins, which hinder His manifest presence in our situation, are dealt with decisively. It is time to give to God the true worship that He is seeking, but it will only happen when the temple is cleansed along with all the articles of worship.

⚜

E. He recognized the sins of his fathers and repented (verses 6-10)

Another important thing that Hezekiah did as he led his nation into spiritual renewal was to recognize the sins of his fathers and repent of them. He consciously and deliberately broke with the prevailing circumstances that he had inherited from his fathers.

Before we can truly experience revival we must seek to identify where our predecessors have failed God and repair the breach. Oftentimes we will be called upon to confess sins that we did not commit personally, but which have caused the work of the Lord to become stuck in a rut. Hezekiah lamented the sins of his forefathers as he cried out:

> Our fathers have trespassed and done evil in the eyes of the Lord our God: They have forsaken Him, have turned their faces away from the dwelling place of the Lord, and turned their backs on Him. They have also shut up the doors of the vestibule, put out the lamps, and have not burned incense or offered burnt offerings in the holy place of the God of Israel (2 Chronicles 29:8-8).

What a terrible wickedness the fathers committed! They literally shut down the work of the Lord. They completely laid down arms. This may have been a result of the external aggression of the enemies or the internal apathy of the people themselves. However, whatever the reason, they allowed the work of the Lord to come to a standstill, and they were accountable to God for such negligence. The work had completely stopped making progress. In fact, it had declined to the point where nothing at all was happening in the house of the Lord. Does that description fit your personal ministry, or that of your church? If so, only a genuine revival can change such reality.

Have you ever experienced a situation in which you see nothing of spiritual significance happening in the house of the Lord? Are you currently in the midst of a situation like that? Are you in a situation in which people have turned away from the dwelling place of the Lord; in which they have turned their backs on Him? Are you in a situation in which the doors of the temple are shut? The lamp is put out. The incense is not being burnt. No sacrifice is being offered. Are you experiencing a situation like that? If so, then it is time to cry out to the Lord for revival. It is time to repent for this waywardness. It is time to turn from this wickedness of lukewarmness and howl before the Lord for our own sins and for the sins of our predecessors, for nothing will change until sins are recognized and confessed.

There has never been a revival, and there will never be a genuine revival, without the recognition, confession and forsaking of past failures. You may need to rise up and make confessions to God on behalf of your nation, for sins the people committed. You may need to confess the past sins of your organization or denomination for the mistakes they have made in the past. You may need to cry out to God for pardon and mercy because of the sins of your ancestors, not to mention your own sins, which may have been carefully tucked away in a corner. We need a wholesale repentance before God if we are truly going to experience a Holy Ghost revival.

Among the first words that Jesus uttered when He began his public ministry was a call to repentance. If we do not heed His call to repentance, we have nothing else to hear from Him. Repentance must precede revival

Hezekiah turned from the sins of his fathers. Nehemiah cried over the sins of his fathers. Daniel confessed the sins of his past generations. They all made a difference. We will never make a difference if we continue to be satisfied with spiritual mediocrity, and past infidelity. Whenever people are struck with the awfulness of past sins and fail to confess them, including the sins of past generations, revival will tarry. Only when we fall before God in confession and repentance will revival follow. There is no point in simply blaming our fathers. There is no virtue in trying to exempt ourselves. We must accept full responsibility for our spirituality.

We are now responsible to God to make a difference in this generation. We cannot go to God and tell Him that we inherited a bad situation. No. We have to give an account for our stewardship. We must make a difference in our lifetime. That means that if we have inherited a sinful or awkward situation, it is our obligation to correct it, and to do so with the correct attitude. This is the work of the Lord and not the work of man. We are the instruments at such a time as this to make right those things that are wrong.

So, we see that Hezekiah could not remain indifferent to prevailing conditions. He refused to simply blame his fathers. He recognized that he would stand guilty before God, for he realized the one who knows to do right and does not do it is guilty of sin (James 4:17). Therefore, Hezekiah turned around a bad situation for the glory of God. If deep in your spirit you are disturbed by the shallowness and sinfulness that you see around you, you need to realise that God can make a difference through you.

In fact, unless you act, and act speedily, the wrath of God may consume your people. The Bible tells us that because of the sins of the fathers the wrath of God fell upon Judah and Jerusalem. Many fell by the sword, and many of their wives and their sons were taken captive. Could it be that many sons and daughters are in captivity today because of the sins of the fathers? Confession and repentance is the first step to break out of captivity. Could it be that many families, churches, para-church organizations and even denominations are in captivity today because in the past certain ancestors or predecessors missed the move of God's Spirit, made serious mistakes, or deliberately disobeyed the will of God?

It is interesting to note that five of the seven churches mentioned in the book of Revelation were called upon to repent. Sometimes the leaders and members of entire churches, organizations, and ministries need to repent before God for past failures that have not been dealt with, or that have been dealt with improperly.

One of the greatest things that leaders can do for their churches is to admit to members when they have made a mistake and repent of it. However, many times church leaders are too proud to admit that they have made a mistake and so they continue to perpetuate the same evil for generations, to the detriment of the work of the Lord. It could be that there are circumstances in your life or ministry that need to be revisited, and set right. You may need to forgive someone who has offended you in the past. You may need to apologise to someone that you have wronged. You may need to go and make restitution for a past failure or bad judgement. Only then will you experience the liberation that comes with revival.

F. He renewed the Covenant with the God of Israel (verse 10)

Having recognized where his predecessors went wrong, and having repented of their sins, Hezekiah was now prepared to remedy the situation. Sometimes, it is necessary to go back to the place where we made a wrong turn in order to get back on the right path. Hezekiah even went further than that. He went back to the very beginning. He went back to the foundation of the relationship between God and the people of Israel. He went back to the covenant God made with Israel. God is a covenant-keeping God.

When God called Abraham to make of him a great nation so that all the nations of the earth would be blessed through him, He made a covenant with Abraham (Genesis 12:1-3). This covenant was renewed to Isaac, Jacob and the descendants of Abraham. The theme of covenant runs through the entire Old Testament, for it was the foundation of the relationship between God and Israel.

It was the breaking of that covenant which caused the wrath of God to be poured out on His people. Therefore, we hear Hezekiah saying, "now it is in my heart to make a covenant with the Lord God of Israel, that his fierce wrath may turn away from us" (2 Chronicles 29:10). Praise the Lord!

The covenant keeping God will renew the broken covenant. Have you broken your covenant with God? He is waiting to renew that covenant. He is a forgiving God. He says, "if we confess our sins, He is faithful and just to forgive us our sins and to cleanse us from all unrighteousness" (1 John 1:9). The psalmist was able to rejoice in the Lord for the forgiveness of sins: "As far as the east is from the west, So far has he removed our transgressions from us" (Psalm 103:12).

My friend, if you have deviated from the path that the Lord has charted for you, God is waiting for you to return. Today, you can return to God and be renewed in your spirit. David was restored to the Lord after he committed adultery and murder. Hear his prayer of confession in Psalm 51:

> 1 Have mercy upon me, O God,
> According to Your loving kindness;
> According to the multitude of Your tender mercies,
> Blot out my transgressions.
> 2 Wash me thoroughly from my iniquity,
> And cleanse me from my sin.
> 3 For I acknowledge my transgressions,
> And my sin *is* always before me.
> 4 Against You, You only, have I sinned,
> And done *this* evil in Your sight—
> That You may be found just when You speak,
> *And* blameless when You judge.
> 5 Behold, I was brought forth in iniquity,
> And in sin my mother conceived me.
> 6 Behold, You desire truth in the inward parts,
> And in the hidden *part* You will make me to know wisdom.
> 7 Purge me with hyssop, and I shall be clean;
> Wash me, and I shall be whiter than snow.
> 8 Make me hear joy and gladness,
> *That* the bones You have broken may rejoice.
> 9 Hide Your face from my sins,
> And blot out all my iniquities.
> 10 Create in me a clean heart, O God,
> And renew a steadfast spirit within me.
> 11 Do not cast me away from Your presence,
> And do not take Your Holy Spirit from me.
> 12 Restore to me the joy of Your salvation,
> And uphold me *by Your* generous Spirit.

13 *Then* I will teach transgressors Your ways,
And sinners shall be converted to You.
14 Deliver me from the guilt of bloodshed, O God,
The God of my salvation,
And my tongue shall sing aloud of Your righteousness.
15 O Lord, open my lips,
And my mouth shall show forth Your praise.
16 For You do not desire sacrifice, or else I would give *it;*
You do not delight in burnt offering.
17 The sacrifices of God *are* a broken spirit,
A broken and a contrite heart—
These, O God, You will not despise.
18 Do good in Your good pleasure to Zion;
Build the walls of Jerusalem.
19 Then You shall be pleased with the sacrifices of righteousness,
With burnt offering and whole burnt offering;
Then they shall offer bulls on Your altar.

In this powerful, penetrative, penitential psalm, notice that although King David had committed grievous sins in the sight of God, he was renewed when he cried out to God for mercy. David is described in God's book as a man after God's own heart (Acts 13:22). He is a God of renewal. He will renew you, no matter how far you have fallen. He is the God of a second chance.

Several hundred years before the time of Hezekiah God had warned the children of Israel that if they were obedient to Him he would look favourably upon them, multiply them, and confirm His covenant with them (Leviticus 26:9). God promised them great blessings if they were faithful to the covenant. On the other hand, He warned that He would punish them severely if they did not keep His covenant. Listen to this very sobering warning to them:

> But if you do not obey me, and do not observe all these
> commandments, and if you despise my statutes, or if your
> soul abhors my judgments, so that you do not perform all
> my commandments, but break my covenant, I also will do
> this to you: I will even appoint terror over you, wasting
> disease and fever which shall consume the eyes and cause
> sorrow of heart. And you shall sow your seed in vain, for
> your enemies shall eat it. I will set my face against you, and
> you shall be defeated by your enemies. Those who hate you
> shall reign over you, and you shall flee when no one pur-
> sues you (Leviticus 26:14-17).

What these verses show is frightening, but the consequences
described are only a small part of the curse that the Lord warned
them of, if they did not keep the covenant with Him. In fact, the
Lord warned that prolonged disobedience would multiply the
plagues upon them seven times, according to their sins (Leviticus
26:18,21,28). The entire twenty-sixth chapter of Leviticus addresses the blessing of obedience and the curse of disobedience. However, it is encouraging to read in verse forty of the same chapter
that confession will lead to the renewal of the covenant. The Lord
said concerning them:

> But if they confess their iniquity and the iniquity of their
> fathers, with their unfaithfulness in which they were un-
> faithful to me, and that they also have walked contrary to
> Me...then I will remember My covenant with Jacob, and
> My covenant with Isaac and My covenant with Abraham I
> will remember: I will remember the Land.

But in God's working, doom prophesied is not always applied. When sin is confessed and forsaken the Lord renews the
covenant. He does not discard the covenant. Are you in need of
spiritual renewal? God is willing to renew a right spirit within you.

He is faithful, and He will renew and restore you to worship and service, if you would only confess your failure and cast yourself upon His mercy.

G. He revived Celebration of Passover (verses 21-27)

After ensuring that the conditions were right for true worship, King Hezekiah summoned the people to gather for the celebration of the Passover. When the conditions are right, celebrations will be inevitable in the house of the Lord. When the house of the Lord is in order, God's glory will be manifested. When the house of the Lord is in order there will be great rejoicing in the house, even in the midst of terrific storms and turbulent waters.

Rejoicing in God's house is not based upon external circumstances. When God's people are experiencing genuine revival there will be great rejoicing in the body, although this may be preceded by, or even accompanied by, great distress. Like Job, we will be able to say: "though He slay me, yet will I trust Him" (Job 13:15). In 2 Chronicles 30 we have a good picture of the rejoicing that was in the temple after it was cleansed and restored:

> [21] So the Children of Israel who were present at Jerusalem kept the Feast of Unleavened Bread seven days with great gladness; and the Levites and the priests praised the Lord day by day, singing to the Lord, accompanied by loud instruments. [22] And Hezekiah gave encouragement to all the Levites who taught the good knowledge of the Lord; and that ate throughout the feast seven days, offering peace offerings and making confession to the Lord God of their fathers.

²³ Then the whole assembly agreed to keep the feast another seven days, and they kept it another seven days with gladness. ²⁴ For Hezekiah king of Judah gave to the assembly a thousand bulls and ten thousand sheep; and a great number of priests sanctified themselves. ²⁵ The whole assembly of Judah rejoiced, also the priests and the Levites, all the assembly that came from Israel, the sojourners who came from the land of Israel, and those who dwelt in Judah. ²⁶ So there was great joy in Jerusalem, for since the time of Solomon the son of David, king of Israel, there had been nothing like this in Jerusalem. ²⁷ Then the priests, the Levites, arose and blessed the people, and their voice was heard, and their prayer came up to His holy dwelling place, to heaven (2 Chronicles 30:21-27).

Worship on earth, the divine writer shows, will reach into heaven when God's conditions are met. There is a sequence to sublime experience. After the temple is repaired and the doors are reopened, and after the priests and Levites are once again reinstated, and after the filthiness is removed from the holy place, and after sins are recognized and repented of, indeed after the covenant is renewed, then and only then, is there going to be true rejoicing in the house of the Lord. It is only then that worship is going to be sweet. It is only then that the fragrance of worship will go up to God as a sweet- smelling savour. It is only then that the glory of God will be manifested.

We should allow nothing to prevent this aroma of worship from going up to God. When the conditions were right, Hezekiah summoned his people to the celebration of the Passover, the memorial of the great deliverance of God's people from bondage in Egypt.

Hezekiah sent letters to all the people of Judah and the remnants of Israel to come to Jerusalem and worship, for the conditions were once again right for true worship. The people came with great enthusiasm to worship the God of their fathers, the covenant-keeping God. They worshipped God in the celebration of the Passover. The Passover had not been celebrated like that for two hundred years. After they worshipped for the prescribed seven days, they decided to worship for another seven days.

When worship is sweet we don't want to quit: we just want to linger in His presence. When worship is pleasing to God, the worshippers also will enjoy it, not endure it. One of the things that we cannot miss in 2 Chronicles 29 is the emphasis was placed on rejoicing or gladness:

- 30 Moreover King Hezekiah and the leaders commanded the Levites to sing praise to the Lord with the words of David and of Asaph the seer. So they sang praises with *gladness*, and they bowed their heads and worshiped (2 Chronicles 29:30).
- 21 So the children of Israel who were present at Jerusalem kept the Feast of Unleavened Bread seven days with great gladness; and the Levites and the priests praised the Lord day by day, singing to the Lord, accompanied by loud instruments (2 Chronicles 30:21)
- 23 Then the whole assembly agreed to keep the feast another seven days, and they kept it another seven days with *gladness* (2 Chronicles 30:23).

Notice that true joy in worship and service was restored to the house of God, and the nation of Judah. Indeed, the glory of God was restored to the nation. It was time of great rejoicing. In his book Revival: Times of Refreshing, Selwyn Hughes has this to say about the place of rejoicing in revival:

> Let no one think that revival is associated with gloom and heaviness and a downcast spirit. There is always a period of mourning for sin, but this is soon followed by waves of endless delight and joy. It is surely amongst the most tragic misrepresentations of truth when historians write that, in times of revival, Christians act like "dejected melancholiacs." It is a travesty of the true tradition of revival. Revival imparts an immense sense of well-being. It produces a witness in the hearts of believers that all is well within. It makes music inside the soul, and bestows a glad exuberance.[58]

Psalm 86 asks the question of the Lord: "Will You not revive us again, that your people may rejoice in You?" May God restore true joy, enthusiasm, and effervescence to our worship, so that we can enjoy the beauty of His manifest presence and behold His glory. When true worship takes the lead, then true joy will follow. Indeed, the glory of God was restored to Judah.

III

HEZEKIAH'S WARFARE

He Rebelled Against the King of Assyria

"He rebelled against the king of Assyria and did not serve him" (2 Kings 18:7)

¹After these deeds of faithfulness, Sennacherib king of Assyria came and entered Judah; he encamped against the fortified cities, thinking to win them over to himself. ² and when Hezekiah saw that Sennacherib had come, and that his purpose was to make war against Jerusalem, ³ he consulted with his leaders and commanders to stop the waters from the springs which were outside the city; and they helped him. ⁴ Thus many people gathered together who stopped all the springs and the brook that ran through the land, saying, "Why should the kings of Assyria come and find much water?" ⁵ And he strengthened himself, built up all the wall that was broken, raised it up to the towers, and built another wall outside; also he repaired the Millo in the City of David, and made weapons and shields in abundance. ⁶ Then he set military captains over the people, gathered them together to him in the open square of the city gate, and gave them encouragement, saying, ⁷ "Be strong and courageous;

do not be afraid nor dismayed before the king of Assyria, nor before all the multitude that is with him; for there are more with us than with him. [8] "With him is the arm of flesh; but with us is the Lord our God, to help us and to fight our battles." And the people were strengthened by the words of Hezekiah king of Judah (2 Chronicles 32:1-8).

Another very significant thing that King Hezekiah did during his reign was to rebel against the king of Assyria (2 Kings 18:7). He was committed to breaking Assyria's dominance over Judah. This courageous act was critically bound up in renewing Judah's walk and worship. This was because Israel was not able to practice pure covenant faith in Yahweh while being a vassal of Assyria. If Assyria had domination over Judah, then Judah would at least have had to give formal allegiance to the gods of Assyria, and Hezekiah was not prepared to stoop to such compromise. Therefore, he was prepared to face the super-power, Assyria, in a battle for his faith. In the book, *Old Testament Survey*, by LaSor, Hubbard, and Bush we learn:

> ...in the ancient Near East, vassal states normally were required to observe their masters' religious practices along with their own."[59]

Hezekiah, therefore, had no option but to combine warfare with his walk and his worship. Anyone who is committed to walking right and worshipping right will of necessity be involved in warfare with the forces of darkness, for there is still an evil army relentlessly opposing anyone and anything dedicated to glorifying God. We do not have to initiate warfare, but when we are passionate about glorifying God through our walk and our worship, the Devil will take the war to us.

Verse one of our text begins with the words "After these deeds of faithfulness..." These words underscore the fact that the work Hezekiah was doing was pleasing to God. There is no doubt that he was doing a magnificent work in Judah. That work caused him to be remembered as the King who led his nation in "the most extensive reform in the history of Judah."[60]

Although he was only twenty-five years old when he ascended the throne, his reign led to a glorious reformation in Judah. He succeeded in propelling his backslidden nation from the pathetic plains of mediocrity, apathy and idolatry to the hills of fervency in worship and service. His reign resulted in renewal, restoration and revival in Judah. Worship was once again elevated to national prominence and the people were once again enjoying worship. Great things were happening. The work of the Lord was progressing magnificently. Let us remind ourselves of the faithful deeds of Hezekiah:

Hezekiah Related Correctly to God—(His Walk was Right)
* He did that which was right in the sight of the Lord
* He removed Idolatry
* He re-examined his heritage
* He relied on God
* He resolutely followed the Lord
* He rebelled against the King of Assyria

Hezekiah Restored God's glory to Judah—(His Worship was Right)
* He repaired the Temple
* He reopened the doors of the temple that his father had closed

- He reinstated the priests and the Levites
- He removed the filthiness from the holy place
- He recognized the sins of his father and repented
- He renewed the covenant with God
- He revived the celebration of Passover

So, there we have it. Hezekiah's walk was right. Hezekiah's worship was right. The king was doing a fantastic job in the name of the Lord. But note: it was after these things that the enemy came. And notice how the enemy came. He came with a wicked intention to destroy the fortified cities, and to take Judah for himself. There is no question about it, whenever and wherever God is doing a great work, the Devil is going to come. He is going to attack with intensity. We must expect him, lest we be caught unaware. The only way we will not have to face his attack is if we are not doing anything significant for God. The Devil will attack anything and anyone that is dedicated to the glory of God. Everything that threatens his Kingdom of Darkness will attract his malicious response.

But we can be assured that "when the enemy comes in like a flood, the Spirit of the Lord will lift up a standard against him" (Isaiah 59:19). Therefore, we are always faced with the option, either to compromise and settle for the mediocre in the work of God, or to fortify ourselves to face the enemy in high-level combat. For the dedicated child of God the choice is clear, when the Devil puts on the fire, it is time to intensify prayer, so that the Lord will fight the battle for us.

George Verwer cautions us in his book, *Out of the Comfort Zone*: "If revival hits your church or region or university, there will be more intense spiritual warfare the very next day."[61] He further says that in the time of revival "there may even be greater heart-breaks and disappointments than before it came."[62] We cannot get very far in the work of the Lord without facing spiritual warfare. Revival time is warfare time. The Devil will seek to do everything to stop the advance of the gospel. But we must resist him in the name of the Lord. Leonard Ravenhill said: "when God opens the window of heaven to bless us, the devil will open the door of hell to blast us."[63] However, the blastings of hell cannot overcome the blessings of heaven.

Anyone who is committed to walking right and worshipping right has no option but to practice, as well, how to engage in spiritual warfare right. We must learn to withstand the forces of evil by appropriating the victory of the Cross of Jesus Christ. If we have a passion to live holy lives and to serve God faithfully, the evil forces of darkness that relentlessly oppose the glory of God will inevitably seek to frustrate us. The Bible clearly encourages us to understand that our real struggle is not against human beings but against principalities, powers, rulers of darkness and spiritual wickedness in high places (Ephesians 6:10). The increasing awareness of supernatural forces in our world is a reality of our time. In his book, *The Adversary*, Mark I. Bubeck makes this poignant remark:

> More rapidly than most of us realise, the questions people ask and the philosophies people believe are changing. No longer is the main debate of men concerned with whether you are a supernaturalist or a non-supernaturalist. Today man's debate centers upon whether you are a "biblical supernaturalist," or an "investigating supernaturalist" who wants to experiment with occult phenomena or in the various branches of sorcery and witchcraft.[64]

Faced with this reality, it is time to heed the Word that says: "Submit to God, resist the devil and he shall flee from you"(James 4:7). When we submit to God and resist the Devil, we have a promise that he shall flee from us. This is because Jesus Christ has already disarmed principalities and powers, and made a public spectacle of them, triumphing over them in the cross (Colossians 2:15). It is still Jesus' purpose to destroy the works of the devil (John 3:8).

Although Hezekiah's walk was right and his worship was right he could not be naive about the enemy's attacks. His warfare also had to be right. Hezekiah stopped paying allegiance to Assyria. He stopped paying the annual tribute. If we are going to wage warfare against the forces of hell, we cannot have any allegiance to them. It is time to stop paying tributes to the Devil. Even tributes that are being paid for three or four generations must now be terminated, right away. They must come to an end, for it is revival time.

We must give to the Devil only what God gives to him. We must give the Devil hell. Carman says, when he comes to you and tells you about your past, tell him about his future.[65] The king of Assyria used various strategies to prevent King Hezekiah from doing God's work in Judah. Let us look at the various tactics that Sennacherib, king of Assyria, used against Hezekiah:

- He tried to jeer him, belittle him and discourage him (2 Kings 18:19-20)
- He tried to discredit him and turn his own people against him. (18:22)
- He tried to invoke fear in him by threatening him (18:27)

- He tried to make an alliance with him (18:31)
- He tried to bribe him with impressive promises (18:31-32)
- He resorted to open confrontation and attack against him.

Clearly then, the Devil will use every means possible to prevent us from doing the work of God. Sometimes he will come as a friend, and at other times he will come as a foe. We must be aware of the Devil's strategies or devices (2 Corinthians 2:11). When one strategy does not succeed he will employ another.

All the tactics that the king of Assyria, Sennacherib, used against Hezekiah failed. He therefore resorted to open confrontation. Sennacherib left a record inscribed on a hexagonal clay prism with details of his eight campaigns. Among other things, he said, regarding Hezekiah: "He himself I shut up like a caged bird within Jerusalem, his royal city"[66] Yes, he was boasting how he locked up Hezekiah in Jerusalem like a bird in a cage. And it is true that at times the Devil might seem to succeed in having us locked in like a bird in a cage.

However, the important thing is what we are doing in the cage when the enemy has us like a bird. Hezekiah was not fretting and whining inside that cage. He was strengthening himself in the Lord and preparing for war. Let us look at the text to see how Hezekiah prepared himself to face the attack of the enemy and learn some important lessons that we can apply to spiritual warfare. It has been said that, "the most constant activity of people living in the world of the Bible in Old Testament times, next to sustaining

life by labour, was warfare."[67] I believe that the physical wars of the
Old Testament may serve to instruct us, as we engage the enemy in
spiritual warfare in our time.

A. He saw the enemy (verse 2)

In 2 Chronicles 32:2 we learn that Hezekiah "saw that the
enemy had come." One of the greatest dangers that we can face is
to be under attack from the Devil and be unaware of it. That is why
the Apostle Paul gives the warning: "Be sober, be vigilant; because
your adversary the devil walks about like a roaring lion, seeking
whom he may devour" (1 Peter 5:8). Many times when people are
under attack from the forces of evil, they tend to blame it on other
human beings and circumstances. However, we need to remember
that we do not wrestle against flesh and blood but against principalities, powers, rulers of darkness and spiritual wickedness in high
places (Ephesians 6:10).

It was a great advantage for Hezekiah in that he saw that the
enemy had come. He also knew for what purpose he had come.
According to verses one and two, Hezekiah knew that the Devil
had come to fight (*milchama*) against Jerusalem and take the city
for himself. When the Devil comes, he does so neither to entertain
nor to occupy space. He comes to wage war against everything
that is dedicated to the glory of God. He comes to kill, steal and
to destroy (John 10:10). Whether he comes subtly, or with open
confrontation, the Devil seeks to capture ground for himself.

In the same way that Sennacherib came to take over Jerusalem for himself, the Devil come to take over our lives, our families, our ministries, our communities, and our nations. And, he will succeed if we do not resist him in the name and power and blood of our Lord Jesus Christ. Once again the Word of God assures us that when we submit to God and resist the Devil then he will have to flee from us (James 4:7).

B. He sought help from his people (verse 3)

Having seen that the enemy had come against him with a great multitude and with a very clear purpose to capture Jerusalem, Hezekiah realized that as king, he had to take some deliberate and decisive actions. The first among these actions that he took was to *seek help* from his people: "He consulted with his leaders and commanders...and they helped him" (verse 3)._We cannot fight this battle alone. We need one another. We need unity to face the enemy. Jesus tells us in Matthew 12:25: "every kingdom divided against itself is brought to desolation, and every city or house divided against itself will not stand." We need the help from the Body of Christ. The Bible says: "For waging war you need guidance, and for victory many advisors" (Proverbs 24:6 NIV). The metaphors of the church as Body, Temple and Household tell us that we must work with each other to accomplish our mission and fulfil our purpose. According to Howard Hendricks, "a person trying to make it on their own is an accident waiting to happen."[68]

We all have different gifts and so we need to complement each other. We are members of the Body of Christ, and we all have different roles to play so that the Body may function effectively. None of us can fulfil our calling and realize our full potential independently. We need to be kind enough to help our brothers and sisters where they need help, and we need to be humble enough to receive help from the Body of Christ. It is high hypocrisy when we pretend that all is well, when we know that we are in desperate need of help. Someone has wittingly said that the worst tense in the English language is *pretense*.

We need one another desperately in the Body of Christ, as we unite against the Prince of darkness. I learned this lesson in a new dimension when I embarked upon a forty day fast some time ago. When I reached about day twenty the spiritual warfare got so intense that had it not been for the grace of God and the support of the Body of Christ, I could have been destroyed. I was then admonished by two of our personal intercessors, Ken and Eileen Terroade, to always have someone fasting with me when I go on extended fasts. The next time I went on a 21 day fast I had my wife, Velda, and brother, Donovan, fast with me. God has taught us that we need to have a group of intercessors praying for us as we do the work of the Lord for we must engage principalities and powers as we do the work of God. Jesus said:

> Again I say to you that if two of you agree on earth concerning anything that they ask, it will be done for them by My Father in heaven. For where two or three are gathered together in My name, I am there in the midst of them (Matthew 18:19-20).

The work of the Lord must be carried out in community. We cannot do it alone. Strength is multiplied exponentially when we unite and help each other. Leviticus 27: 8 tells us, "Five of you shall chase a hundred, and a hundred of you shall put ten thousand to flight." Ecclesiastes also bears out this important teaching:

> Two *are* better than one,
> Because they have a good reward for their labor.
> 10 For if they fall, one will lift up his companion.
> But woe to him *who is* alone when he falls,
> For *he has* no one to help him up.
> 11 Again, if two lie down together, they will keep warm;
> But how can one be warm *alone?*
> 12 Though one may be overpowered by another, two can withstand him.
> And a threefold cord is not quickly broken
> (Ecclesiastes 4:9-12).

Hezekiah realized that he needed the help of his princes and his mighty men. He sought their counsel, and it is important to note that, "they helped him" (verse 3). Sometimes pride can cause us to refuse much needed help. That can be dangerous. We will never accomplish anything significant in the kingdom of God without the help of God's people. Any great work of God will involve God's people.

God did not plan His work to be a 'one-man show.' In fact, it is said that one of the marks of a true leader is that when he looks behind him he sees people following. If people are not following then he is only taking a short walk. We must find those persons whom God has ordained and anointed to help us realize the vision that he has given to us for we cannot do it by ourselves. Christians are like a strand of cord. When we are alone the enemy can easily break us, but when we are with others, we are not easily broken. The Devil cannot break the intertwined cords. The Bible says, "a threefold cord is not easily broken" (Ecclesiastes 4:12).

God used Moses' father-in-law, Jethro, to teach him this very important lesson. When Jethro saw how much Moses was doing and the weight of the burden that he was carrying, he gave him the wise counsel to delegate some of his responsibilities:

> 17 So Moses' father-in-law said to him, "The thing that you do *is* not good. 18 Both you and these people who *are* with you will surely wear yourselves out. For this thing *is* too much for you; you are not able to perform it by yourself. 19 Listen now to my voice; I will give you counsel, and God will be with you: Stand before God for the people, so that you may bring the difficulties to God. 20 And you shall teach them the statutes and the laws, and show them the way in which they must walk and the work they must do. 21 Moreover you shall select from all the people able men, such as fear God, men of truth, hating covetousness; and place *such* over them *to be* rulers of thousands, rulers of hundreds, rulers of fifties, and rulers of tens. 22 And let them judge the people at all times. Then it will be *that* every great matter they shall bring to you, but every small matter they themselves shall judge. So it will be easier for you, for they will bear *the burden* with you. 23 If you do this thing, and God *so* commands you, then you will be able to endure, and all this people will also go to their place in peace."
> 24 So Moses heeded the voice of his father-in-law and did all that he had said. 25 And Moses chose able men out of all Israel, and made them heads over the people: rulers of thousands, rulers of hundreds, rulers of fifties, and rulers of tens. 26 So they judged the people at all times; the hard

cases they brought to Moses, but they judged every small
case themselves (Exodus 18:17-26).

So, we have seen that Hezekiah saw that the enemy had come
with the wicked intention to take over Jerusalem for himself. He
sought help from his princes and his mighty men. But, he did more
than that. There are times when waging war against the Enemy we
have to do something more.

C. He stopped the water supply to the enemy (verses 3-4).

The text tells us in verses three and four that he

> ...consulted with his leaders and commanders to stop the
> water from the springs which were outside the city; and
> they helped him. Thus many people gathered together who
> stopped all the springs and the brook that ran through the
> land, saying, "Why should the kings of Assyria come and
> find much water?

Hezekiah could not find any good reason why he should allow the water from his city to quench the thirst of the enemies who
were outside the city waiting to come in and destroy them.

He therefore marshaled his army to cut off all water supplies
going to the enemy. This is one of the greatest accomplishments
for which King Hezekiah is remembered. He led his people to dig
a tunnel of 1,777 feet through solid rock to connect the Gihon
Spring to the pool of Silome.[69] Thus, he prevented the enemies
from being refreshed by the waters of the holy city.

What a wonderful lesson for us who too many times do the contrary. So often we fatten the enemy to better enable him to come and destroy us. We feed him with gossip, lies, backbiting, stealing, sexual immorality, dissention and a host of other sins. We invite him in, entice him in, and give him a pathway and even a platform from which to operate. Sometimes we even squander our scarce resources on things that enhance the Devil's programme. Paul admonishes us that we must not give any place to the Devil (Ephesians 4:27). Someone has said that if we give the Devil an inch he will take a yard. Another person puts it differently: if you continue giving the Devil inch-by-inch he will eventually become a ruler!

We must cut off all supply to the Enemy. Let him stay out there and starve. Don't give him any space in which to manoeuvre. Lock him out and leave him out. Let him stay out. If you have been guilty of entertaining the Devil it is time to cut off the water supply. We must cut off the supply of the Enemy: the world, the flesh, and the Devil. The Bible warns: "Do not love the world or the things in the world. If anyone loves the world, the love of the Father is not in him." (1 John 2:15) It is time to sever any allegiance to the Enemy. Just as King Hezekiah stopped paying the annual tribute to Assyria we must stop paying all tribute whatsoever to the Devil.

D. He strengthened himself (verse 5)

Another important thing that King Hezekiah did in the time of warfare was that he "strengthened himself" (verse 5). We cannot afford to be weak in the time of spiritual warfare. We all stand under the divine imperative to be strong (*endunamousthe*—literally to put on the dunamis) in the Lord and in the power (*kratei*) of His might (*ischuos*) (Ephesians 6:10). We cannot afford to be weak and "wisshy washy" in these days. It is time for us to strengthen ourselves in the Lord. It is our solemn responsibility to do those things that will make us strong in the Lord: prayer and fasting, study of God's word, and fellowship with other Christians.

The Bible clearly teaches that it is in the Lord that we find this strength. The word rendered "be strong" in Ephesians 6:10 is the same word used in 1 Timothy 1:12 in which Paul says: "I thank Christ Jesus our Lord who has enabled me (strengthened me), because He counted me faithful, putting me into the ministry." Paul also boldly declared in Philippians 4:13: "I can do all things through Christ who strengthens me" (see also 2 Timothy 4:17).

Indeed, God is our refuge and strength, a very present help in times of trouble. But it is those who wait upon the Lord that will renew their strength. They will mount up with wings like eagles, run and not be weary, walk and not faint (Isaiah 40:31). Joshua was told to be strong and of good courage when it was time to enter the Promised Land. We have to be strong and courageous to enter our God-given possessions for Christ. The prophet Haggai told the people to be strong as they rebuilt the temple of the Lord after the exile. The word of the Lord says:

> Yet now be strong, O Zerubbabel, saith the Lord; and be strong O Joshua, son of Josedech, and be strong , all ye people of the land, saith the Lord, and work, for I am with you, saith the Lord of host (Haggai 2:4).

Any building or rebuilding that is being done must be done in the strength of the Lord.

The Apostle charged the Ephesian church to be strong in the Lord by putting on the full armour of God. We must fortify ourselves to stand against the wiles of the Devil. We must have our feet shod with the preparation of the gospel of peace. We must be equipped with the helmet of salvation, the shield of faith, the breastplate of righteousness, the sword of the spirit and prayer with supplication. We can and should appropriate the God- given resources that will render us strong in the Lord. The prophet Isaiah reminds:

> 29 He gives power to the weak,
> And to *those who have* no might He increases strength.
> 30 Even the youths shall faint and be weary,
> And the young men shall utterly fall,
> 31 But those who wait on the Lord
> Shall renew *their* strength;
> They shall mount up with wings like eagles,
> They shall run and not be weary,
> They shall walk and not faint.
> (Isaiah 40:29-31).

Yes, it is only those who give themselves to waiting upon God who will discover this new strength in the Lord. Do you feel weak and weary, tired and discouraged? It is time to call upon the Lord for new strength. We cannot afford to be weak and feeble for it is warfare time, and warfare requires the strength and courage of the Lord. In his book, *Overcoming the Adversary*, Mark Bubeck says:

Hope and courage are vital words in spiritual warfare.
Courage is not only necessary in facing our relentless foe,
but it is also the believer's purchased possession. Satan
would like nothing better than to fill believers with dread
of him and his kingdom. If he can keep his work shrouded
in an aura of mystery or if he can cloak his programs with
sensationalized hocus-pocus in the minds of believers, Satan will have accomplished one of his chief aims.[70]

We can be strong in the Lord, not because of our own effort but because of the Finished Work of Jesus Christ in his death,
burial and resurrection. We can face the Devil in the resurrection
power of Jesus Christ.

E. He sealed up the broken walls (verse 5)

Another important thing that King Hezekiah did was that he
sealed up the broken walls (verse 5). It is important to seal up all
the cracks in the wall, for it is precisely at these vulnerable places
that the Devil will attack. It is often said that a chain is as strong as
its weakest link. When there is a crack in the wall the whole church
is vulnerable. It was Achan alone who cracked up during the con-
quest of the great city of Jericho. Yet, because of it, the entire army
lost the next battle with Ai, which was much smaller than Jericho
(Joshua 7).

It certainly does not make sense for the rest of the body to
criticise, deny or slight the crack. We cannot afford to criticise or
curse the crack. We must correct it. We cannot afford to slight the
crack. We must seal the crack. It is not even enough to rebuke the

crack. We must remedy the crack. The Bible tells us in Galatians 6:1 how we are to deal with the crack:

> Brethren, if a man is overtaken in any trespass, you who are spiritual restore such a one in a spirit of gentleness, considering yourself lest you also be tempted.

Since it is the whole body that is affected by the crack, the best thing to do as soon as a crack is observed is to seal it up. If you notice a crack in your life, please attend to it immediately, because it is not only making you vulnerable, but also the whole church. Do not be comfortable with the crack or condone the crack. Some people overlook the crack and even explain away the crack by saying "that's how I am. It is the month that I was born."

However, those of us who are "born again" cannot tolerate cracks in our lives for we are now a part of the new creation and brand new people in Christ. As new creations in Christ, it is time to seal the crack and cut off the worldly or questionable entertainment. If you entertain the crack, the Devil can enter through the crack, and by that means he will attack, which means, he will kill, steal and destroy (John 10:10). We must neither entertain the crack, nor be entertained by the crack.

The blood of Jesus Christ is able to seal up the cracks in the wall. It is the only agent to remedy the crack. It does not matter how wide the crack is, or how long it has been there. There is a divine remedy for the crack. It is stronger than cement, or glue, or epoxy. It is the incorruptible blood of Jesus Christ.

The story is told of a man who went to the doctor and was given a prescription after he was examined.[71] A few days later his wife turned up at the doctor's office requesting a death certificate. The doctor could not believe that the man had died. He went to the man's house to verify the situation. It was true. The man was dead. The doctor began to look around the house as though he were searching for something special. Finally, he found a package hidden somewhere in the ceiling. The package was unopened. It was the medication that the doctor had prescribed. The doctor said, "This man did not die because of his sickness. He died because he refused to take the remedy." The only remedy for sin is the blood of Jesus Christ and if we do not apply the remedy, the disease of sin will destroy us.

Are there cracks in your life that need to be sealed? It is time to seal every point of entry from the Devil. Look for the cracks in the wall and seal them up, now. If you don't, the crack will crack you up.

F. He secured weapons (verse 5)

Having seen the enemies coming, having sought help from his people, having stopped the water supply to the enemies, and having strengthened himself, Hezekiah was now ready to take another important step: he *secured weapons* (verse 5). The text tells us that he made "darts and shields in abundance" (KJV).

To fight this warfare we need weapons. We cannot fight it bare handed. The weapons of our warfare are not carnal, but mighty in God for pulling down strongholds (2 Corinthians 10:4). "The arms of flesh will fail you. Ye dare not trust your own."[72] The

Bible tells us that Hezekiah made two kinds of weapons, darts and shields. They are rendered in the original as the *shelach* (dart) and the *magen* (shield). The *shelach* was a missile of attack or a spear. It was used to shoot into the camp of the enemy. On the other hand, the *magen* (shield) was a weapon of defence. It was used for protection.

When we wage warfare against the Enemy we must furnish ourselves with defensive weapons as well as offensive weapons. Yes, we must protect ourselves, even while attacking. We are called to protect our turf and to attack the Enemy's turf. We must fire shots into the camp of the Enemy. Christianity is a missionary movement and we are called to go into the camp of the Enemy and establish the Kingdom of God, in process, taking back what the Devil has stolen from us. We must invade Enemy territory, confront and bind the Strong Man and plunder his house (Matthew 12:29).

We are expected to take people out of the Kingdom of Darkness and bring them into the Kingdom of Light. This can only be done through serious spiritual warfare. The Devil will not give up his subjects without a fight. Many are waiting to be delivered from the land of bondage, and taken to the Promised Land.

Hezekiah secured weapons, and he did so in abundance. Let us now arm ourselves with the weapons that God has made available to us. Once again, Ephesians 6 tells us of the weapons that we need the belt of truth, the breastplate of righteousness, feet shod with the preparation of the gospel of peace, the shield of faith, the helmet of salvation, the sword of the spirit, which is the Word of God and prayers intensified with supplication. Spiritual warfare must be fought with spiritual weapons. Do not lower your standards to fight spiritual warfare with worldly and fleshly weapons.

Stick to the weapons that the Lord has blessed. They will always be effective though they may be regarded as "foolishness" in the eyes of the world. We must overcome by using the weapons of righteousness. In everything our warfare must be carried out in love for God and for our fellowmen. Our real enemies are not human beings, so we must be committed to loving people, even those who curse us and despitefully use us (Luke 5:22) for love is more powerful than hate.

※

G. He set captains of war over the people (verse 6)

Another important thing that King Hezekiah did in the time of warfare was to set captains of war over the people. Verse six tells us, "He set military captains over the people." Not everyone is trained in warfare but everyone needs to be protected. Those who are more advanced in the things of the Lord must provide covering for the younger and less mature ones. This is partly why the cell group system is so important.

People who are more mature in the Lord must see it as their responsibility to pray for, and disciple, those who are less mature in the Lord. Just as Hezekiah set captains of war over the people we must set prayer warriors over our people. We must do this because the Devil is a roaring lion walking about, seeking whom he may devour (1 Peter 5:8). There needs to be intercessors in the church that will carry the burdens of others, as the Old Testament priests carried the names of the twelve tribes upon their breasts. We need more people like Anna of old, who "did not depart from the temple, but served God with fastings and prayers night and day" (Luke 2:37).

The Apostle Paul admonishes us: "I exhort first of all that supplications, prayers, intercessions, and giving of thanks be made for all men" (1 Timothy 2:1). Are there persons whom the Lord has placed on your heart to intercede for? Please do it faithfully. Your prayers may save such a person's life and testimony. In his book, Prayer Shield, Dr. C. Peter Wagner has placed intercessors in four groups: General Intercessors, Crisis Intercessors, Personal Intercessors and Warfare Intercessors.[73]

General Intercessors are those who will remember to address any prayer requests that they become aware of. They can be relied upon to pray for items mentioned for prayer in the bulletin.

Crisis Intercessors are especially motivated to pray in times of crisis. The Spirit of God often moves these persons to pray for others when they are facing difficulties.

Personal Intercessors are those whom God has given the special assignment to pray for particular persons. For example, the Lord may place a missionary on your heart to pray for faithfully and consistently. Those who are in the forefront of the battle need Personal Intercessors.

Finally, Warfare Intercessors are those who are called to face the Devil in head-on confrontation, in high level combat. Not everyone is prepared for this level of intercession and it must not be entered into casually. Military captains are urgently needed today to watch over and pray earnestly for the rest of the Body.

When Hezekiah saw the enemy coming, he sought help from his people. He stopped the water supply to the enemy. He strengthened himself. He sealed up the broken walls. He secured weapons, and he set captains of war over the people. Yet, his strategy was not complete for we cannot face warfare without a Word from the Lord.

H. He spoke the Word of God to the people (verses 6-8)

Therefore, in verse six we see that he spoke the Word of God to the people. In times of warfare, we need to hear from God. We need a Word from God. If we don't hear from God, What will we do? Warfare calls for precise directions from our Commander in Chief, Jesus Christ. It is the Word of God that is a lamp unto our feet and a light unto our path (Psalm 119:105). It is the Word of God that is our two-edged sword.

In fact, the Bible tells us that the Word is living and powerful, and sharper than any two edged sword, piercing even to the division of soul and spirit, and of the joints and marrow, and is a discerner of the thoughts and intents of the heart (Hebrew 4:12). It is the sword of the Spirit (Ephesians 6:17). We cannot engage in warfare without it.

It was the Word that Jesus used when he engaged the Devil in a high level combat in the wilderness, and it is the Word that will help us when the Devil comes against us today. Hezekiah had to deliver the unadulterated Word of God to the people as they faced the attacks of the enemy. He spoke the Word of God to the people (6b-8). When we face the oppositions and attacks of the Devil, nothing will help us like a Word from the Lord. Whatever form the attacks take, God has a Word to help us.

The enemy had besieged Jerusalem and Hezekiah spoke the Word of God to encourage his people. Let us hear the Word of the Lord that Hezekiah gave to the people, and let us hear it now in our various circumstances and take it as a personal word from the Lord. Hear the word of the Lord as it is recorded in 2 Chronicles:

> Be strong and courageous; do not be afraid nor dismayed before the king of Assyria, nor before all the multitude that is with him; for there are more with us than with him. With him is an arm of flesh; but with us is the Lord our God, to help us and to fight our battles." And the people were strengthened by the words of Hezekiah king of Judah (2 Chronicles 32:7:8).

If you are going though warfare, you can embrace this Word from the Lord, for His Word is forever settled in heaven (Psalm 119:89). Take a hold of the Word of God until the Word of God takes a hold of you.

In times of warfare we cannot afford to be weak. The Lord reminds us that we need to be strong and courageous. The Hebrew word khawzak, and its derivatives, are used three times in verses five to seven. The text tells us that Hezekiah "strengthened himself" (verse 5), that he "strengthened" (rendered "repaired") the wall Millo (verse 5), and now that he gave the people a direct encouragement from the Lord to be strong (verse 7).

If we are going to be triumphant in the work of the Lord we must be strong. Someone has said, 'when the going gets tough, the tough get going." We cannot bow under the pressures that the Enemy will try to put us under. We must stand flat-footed against all the attacks of the enemy. We must submit to God, and resist the Devil for we have the assurance from God that he will flee from us (James 4:7). Remember the little chorus so commonly sung in the Caribbean:

> Press along saints; press along, in God's own way.
> Persecution we must bear.
> Trials and crosses in our way.
> But, the hotter the battle, the sweeter the victory.

We must be strong and very courageous. We must not be afraid or dismayed. One of the most frequently used tools in the Devil's tool kit is fear. Fear will immobilize us. Fear will rob us of our blessings and even bring the work of God to a halt. Fear and faith are mutually exclusive. We must hold on to the Word of the Lord in faith. Do not break down, nor give up. We must heed the encouragement to be strong. Why? Because the multitude that is with us is greater than the multitude that is against us. With the Enemy is the arm of flesh, but with us is the Lord our God. Because God is with us we do not have to worry or fret. He promises that He will never leave us, nor forsake us (Hebrews 13:5). His words to Joshua are still relevant to us:

> 6 Be strong and of good courage, for to this people you shall divide as an inheritance the land which I swore to their fathers

to give them. 7 Only be strong and very courageous, that you may observe to do according to all the law which Moses My servant commanded you; do not turn from it to the right hand or to the left, that you may prosper wherever you go. *8* This Book of the Law shall not depart from your mouth, but you shall meditate in it day and night, that you may observe to do according to all that is written in it. For then you will make your way prosperous, and then you will have good success. *9* Have I not commanded you? Be strong and of good courage; do not be afraid, nor be dismayed, for the Lord your God *is* with you wherever you go"(Joshua 1:6-9).

Yes, the Lord is with us. Moreover, the Lord promises that He *will help us* (verse 8). God will not fail us. He will help us. He is our refuge and strength, a very present help in trouble (Psalm 46:1). He will come to our rescue. The psalmist was aware of this help from the Lord:

> May He send you help from the sanctuary,
> And strengthen you out of Zion;
> (Psalm 20:2)

> Our soul waits for the Lord;
> He *is* our help and our shield.
> (Psalm 33:20)

> 1 I will lift up my eyes to the hills—
> From whence comes my help?
> 2 My help *comes* from the Lord,
> Who made heaven and earth.
> (Psalm 121:1-2)

> 8 Our help *is* in the name of the Lord,
> Who made heaven and earth.
> (Psalm 124:8)

The prophet Isaiah spoke of this help from the Lord in Isaiah 41:10-14

> 10 Fear not, for I *am* with you;
> Be not dismayed, for I *am* your God.
> I will strengthen you,
> Yes, I will help you,
> I will uphold you with My righteous right hand.'
> 11 "Behold, all those who were incensed against you
> Shall be ashamed and disgraced;
> They shall be as nothing,
> And those who strive with you shall perish.
> 12 You shall seek them and not find them—
> Those who contended with you.
> Those who war against you
> Shall be as nothing,
> As a nonexistent thing.
> 13 For I, the Lord your God, will hold your right hand,
> Saying to you, 'Fear not, I will help you.'
> 14 "Fear not, you worm Jacob,
> You men of Israel!
> I will help you," says the Lord
> And your Redeemer, the Holy One of Israel.

Hear the exhortation to the people of God who were faced with hardships, even to the point that some were thinking of giving up the faith:

> Let us therefore come boldly to the throne of grace, that we may obtain mercy and find grace to help in time of need (Hebrews 4:16).
> For in that He Himself has suffered, being tempted, He is able to aid those who are tempted (Hebrews 2:18).

Therefore, we can be encouraged, for help is available today. Remember that the Holy Spirit is the *paracletos* (The One who comes alongside to help). Hold out my friend, help is on the way, for God is sending help from His sanctuary.

The Lord promises to help us. He promises to Himself fight our battles. As long as we are trusting in the Lord, He will take on our battles. He Himself will deal with our enemies. We only have to be faithful to Him. It does not matter how great the multitude is that is against us. The Word of God assures us that the multitude that is with us is greater than the multitude that is against us. The Bible points out clearly that with the Enemy is the arm of flesh, but with us is the Lord (*Yahweh*) our God (*Eloheeynuw*).

When we think of who is with us, even the weak can say he is strong. It is Yahweh (Jehovah) who is with us. It is important to note that help comes from Yahweh (Jehovah). It is not just any god, but Yahweh Himself. Here is what the *Vine's Complete Expository Dictionary of Old and New Testament Words* has this to say about Yahweh (often rendered by the vowel-less word YHWH):

> The divine name YHWH appears only in the Bible. Its precise meaning is much debated. God chose it as His personal name by which He related specifically to His chosen or covenant people. [74]

Praise the Lord! Our help comes from Jehovah, our God. Sometimes, Jehovah is used as part of a compound word to express other names for God.

> In scripture a name is often an expression of the nature,
> of its bearer, describing his character, position, function,
> some circumstances affecting him, or some hope or sorrow
> concerning him"[75]

Here are some of the compound names for God with the name
Jehovah:

Jehovah-Jireh—"God our provider" (Gen. 22:13-14). This testifies
to God's provision.

Jehovah Sabaoth—"The LORD of Hosts." Meaning: Jehovah of the
(heavenly) armies

Jehovah Nissi—"The Lord my Banner" Exodus 17:15, see Hebrew
12:2

Jehovah Rophi—"The Lord who heals you" Exodus 15:26

Jehovah Tzadekenu (Tsidikenu)—"The Lord our Righteousness" Jeremiah 23:6

Jehovah Shalom—"The Lord is peace" Judges 6:24

Jehovah Rohi—"The Lord my shepherd" John 10:14,15

Yes, Jehovah is with us. Jehovah will help and He will fight our
battles. He said to the children of Israel:

> The Lord your God, who goes before you, He will fight for
> you, according to all He did for you in Egypt before your
> eyes (Deuteronomy 1:30).

He also says: "You must not fear them, for the Lord your God Himself fights for you" (Deuteronomy 3:22)

When Moses and the children of Israel stood on the shore of the Red Sea and Pharaoh and his army were pursuing them, it seemed like an impossible situation. It was tragedy. It was sure destruction, it seemed. But, it was God who fought the battle. Moses said to the people: "The Lord (Jehovah) will fight for you, and you shall hold your peace" (Exodus 14:14). The Lord instructed Moses to stretch his rod across the waters, and when Moses obeyed, the Lord made a way in the midst of the Red Sea.

It was the same message that the Lord gave to His people when the people of Moab and Ammon and a host of others came to fight against Jehoshaphat. The prophet Jehezael spoke the following word of encouragement to the people:

> Listen, all you of Judah and you inhabitants of Jerusalem, and you, King Jehoshaphat! Thus says the Lord to you: 'Do not be afraid nor dismayed because of this great multitude, for the battle is not yours, but God's. (2 Chronicles 20:15).

All they were required to do was to praise the Lord, and the Lord Himself fought the battle. You don't need to worry about the battle, just concentrate on the praises; just play the music, play the music sweet, for the Battle is the Lord's. Today, the message is the same. The Word of the Lord will prevail. The Word strengthened Hezekiah and his people in battle. The Word also strengthened Jehoshaphat and his people in battle. The Word can strengthen you and your people in battle today. The Bible tells us that when Hezekiah delivered the Word of the Lord to the people, "they were strengthened by the words of Hezekiah king of Judah" (verse 8).

Indeed, when we have received a word from the Lord we can be strong. When we have a word from God, even the weak can say "I am strong." The Word of God, recorded in the sixty-six canonical books of the Bible, continues to be the powerful infallible Word of God to strengthen us today. May we commit ourselves afresh to feasting upon the Word of God.

I experienced the power of the Word of God in my own life in new dimensions in 1984 when Jamaica Youth for Christ had its Year of the Bible Programme. During that year young people were challenged to commit large portions of Scripture to memory. My involvement in that programme led me to memorize and recite 1100 verses of Scripture (1/8 of the New Testament). The intensive study of the Word significantly enriched my spiritual life. It was during that period of intense Bible Memorization that I got a divine confirmation of a call to Christian Ministry. Feeding upon the Word of God definitely adds vitality to the spiritual life.

Hezekiah used strategy in warfare. The enemy was pressing hard against him. Jerusalem was besieged, and he was locked up in the royal city like a bird in a cage. But, he prepared himself to stand against the wiles or methods of the enemy by taking some very important steps, when he saw the enemy coming. He sought help from his people. He stopped the water supply to the enemy. He strengthened himself. He sealed up the broken walls. He secured weapons. He set captains of war over the people and he spoke the Word of God to them.

His strategy had yet another major ploy, one so important it merits particular focus, for it is the bedrock of revival.

IV

HEZEKIAH'S WARFARE (II)

He Resorted to Fervent Prayer

1 In those days Hezekiah was sick and near death. And Isaiah the prophet, the son of Amoz, went to him and said to him, "Thus says the Lord: 'Set your house in order, for you shall die and not live.'"

2 Then he turned his face toward the wall, and prayed to the Lord, saying 3"Remember now, O Lord, I pray, how I have walked before you in truth and with a loyal heart, and have done what was good in Your sight." And Hezekiah wept bitterly.

4 And it happened, before Isaiah had gone out into the middle court, that the word of the Lord came to him, saying,

5 "Return and tell Hezekiah the leader of my people, 'Thus says the Lord, the God of David your father: "I have heard your prayer, I have seen your tears; surely I will heal you. On the third day you shall go up to the house of the Lord.

6 And I will add to your days fifteen years. I will deliver you and this city from the hand of the king of Assyria; and I will defend this city for my own sake, and for the sake of My servant David." (2 Kings 20:1-6)

In the story so far we have seen how King Hezekiah related correctly to God, how he restored God's glory to Judah, and how he rebelled against the king of Assyria. We will now look at how he resorted to fervent prayer.

We cannot get very far without prayer. Prayer is the foundation of any revival. In his book, *Seasons of Revival: Understanding the Appointed Times of Spiritual Refreshing*, Frank Damazio says:

> There has always been a spirit of prayer and intercession associated with spiritual awakening, both in Scripture and in history. Revival is preceded by prayer, birthed through intercession, and sustained by fervent persevering prayer. Prayer is the central living element to every spiritual awakening and every moving of the Holy Spirit.[76]

He further relates the importance of prayer to the church:

> The church may be like a well designed machine with intricate parts of all sizes and shapes designed and assembled to work smoothly, yet without lubrication these parts will destroy each other. Prayer is God's oil of lubrication for His church.[77]

Hezekiah faced a situation that needed spiritual lubrication. The nation of Judah was under siege. The Assyrians were outside the walls of Jerusalem waiting to come in and take over Judah for themselves. And Hezekiah did not have the military might of King David nor King Solomon. From all natural indications, he was in a precarious position. Here is a man of God who had set himself to serve his Lord whole-heartedly. Yet, he was now in great trouble.

In addition to the attacks of Assyria, Hezekiah was sick and at the point of death. O how the challenges of life seem to come at the most inappropriate and inconvenient times in our lives! Yet, we must always persevere and conquer. Perhaps we need to be reminded that, "missions is carried out in the context of change, crisis, and the unexpected turns of life"[78]

Whatever happens, the work of the Lord must continue. The victory of the cross must be established. Interestingly, there is evidence that the Lord's work often mushrooms under the most adverse circumstances. Why should trouble come when we have set ourselves to serve the Lord? I believe that sometimes God deliberately sets us up so that we can experience His power and see His glory manifested in our situations. Jim Cymbala says:

> Trouble is one of God's greatest servants because it reminds us how much we continually need the Lord. Otherwise, we tend to forget about entreating him. For some reason we want to carry on by ourselves."[79]

The Bible tells us that all who desire to live godly in Christ Jesus will suffer persecution (2 Timothy 3:12).

However, persecution cannot stop the advance of the Kingdom of God. It only fuels the fire. Persecution has never quenched the fire of the Church, and it never will. The Bible clearly points out that the more the Egyptians oppressed the children of Israel while they were in Egypt, the more the Children of Israel increased in numbers. The Church is like that. The early disciples rejoiced in that they suffered on account of Jesus. The Apostle Peter says:

> 6 In this you greatly rejoice, though now for a little while, if need be, you have been grieved by various trials, 7 that the genuineness of your faith, *being* much more precious than gold that perishes, though it is tested by fire, may be found to praise, honor, and glory at the revelation of Jesus Christ, 8 whom having not seen you love. Though now you do not see *Him,* yet believing, you rejoice with joy inexpressible and full of glory, 9 receiving the end of your faith—the salvation of *your* souls (1Peter 1:6-9).

Persecution, trials and suffering often propel us to intensity in prayer. But, nowadays, the Church in the West seems to have a totally different theology of suffering from that of the Early Church and from that of the persecuted church, especially in the East where millions are laying down their lives for Christ. However, it is a noted fact that where the Church is being persecuted, commitment is not casual, devotion is not half-hearted, and prayer is not superficial. When the Devil puts us under fire we have no option but to intensify our prayer. We must not quit. We must not compromise. We must intensify prayer.

When Hezekiah was in much trouble he prayed more. Look at how much trouble he was in. His nation was surrounded by the Assyrian army. He himself was struggling with severe physical affliction. What did he do in that time of great distress? He did not simply worry. He did not curse his enemy, his people, or himself. He did not succumb to discouragement. He turned to the Lord for help. He resorted to fervent prayer.

And, it was not as a last resort either. When Hezekiah received the letter of threat from the messengers of the enemy he "went up to the house of the Lord, and spread it before the Lord"(2

Kings 19:14). When trouble comes, let us not be too afraid, or too slothful to spread it before the Lord. Like Joseph Scriven, the song-writer, I believe that many times we have to confess:

> O what peace we often forfeit
> O What needless pain we bear,
> All because we do not carry
> Everything to God in prayer.[80]

Jim Cymbala reminds us that the "the feature that is supposed to distinguish Christian churches, Christian people and Christian gatherings is the aroma of prayer.[81]

Prayer is a tremendous privilege that the child of God has. It is marvellous to think that finite human beings can communicate with the infinite God. We can use the privilege of prayer at any time, from any location, and we need no cellular phones. We will never get a recording advising us that our party is out of range, or has turned off the instrument. We need to go through no operator, for we already have one mediator between God and man, the man Christ Jesus (1 Timothy 2:5).

We can log on to God at anytime and we need no server for we already have the Saviour. No wonder the psalmist exclaimed, "I will call upon the Lord who is worthy to be praised, so shall I be saved from my enemies" (Psalm 18:3).

In his book, *Breaking Strongholds: How Spiritual Warfare Sets Captives Free*, Tom White writes:

> We can analyse our problems, share them with others, and resolve to turn over a new leaf, but the most powerful agent of change is the Holy Spirit moving in response to a prayer of authority.[82]

God facilitates our prayer. We merely need to pray. "Let us therefore come boldly to the throne of grace, that we may obtain mercy and find grace to help in times of need" (Hebrews 4:16).

I believe that the greatest problem of the church today is that we have too many cold-hearted, dry-eyed Christians. We have too many Christians who have no clue about what it is to prevail in prayer. Leonard Ravenhill is right when he says, "Surely revival delays, because prayer decays."[83] In his book *Engaging the Powers: Discernment and Resistance in a World of Domination,* Walter Wink reminds us: "History belongs to the intercessors, who believe the future into being."[84] He puts it pointedly when he states:

> Even a small number of people, firmly committed to the new inevitability on which they fix their imaginations, can decisively affect the shape the future takes. The shapers of the future are the intercessors, who call out of the future the longed-for new present.[85]

Hezekiah was certainly someone who had that kind of concept of prayer. Let us look at the prayer of King Hezekiah and learn some principles that will fuel our own prayer life. I believe that we can find some lessons here that will help us to pray the kind of prayer that will help us to prepare for God's promised and soon coming global revival. Let us first of all look at the intensity of Hezekiah's asking[86], as we examine Hezekiah's prayer.

A. He demonstrated the intensity of the asking (verses 2-3)

The intensity of his prayer may be deduced from the fact that Hezekiah "turned his face toward the wall, and prayed to the Lord" (2 Kings 20:2). He refused to be distracted by all the incidentals around him. He had no appetite for the things around him. He shut out all other activities so that he could pray to the Lord without disturbance. Sometimes, God has to use tragedy to get our undivided attention, though that was not necessarily the case for Hezekiah.

Hezekiah was the leader of a nation that was facing warfare, and he himself was sick, yet he found time to pray. The truth is that he had no option. He either prayed or perished. It is a real tragedy when we become so perpetually busy that we cannot find time to pray. Too often, we become so caught up with the urgent that we neglect the important. If we get too busy to pray we are too busy indeed!

Hezekiah, however, did not let that happen to him. He made time for prayer. He turned his face to the wall and prayed to the Lord. He was serious about prayer. The Bible also tells us that "Hezekiah wept bitterly" (verse 3). When we weep in prayer we are deep in prayer. Most of us need to be more intense in prayer. The Kings James Version of the Bible says, "Hezekiah wept sore." The New International Version and the New King James Version both translate that comment: "Hezekiah wept bitterly." A literal translation of the Hebrew is: "Hezekiah wept a great weeping." If we put it in Jamaican Creole it will be something to the force of 'Hezekiah ban him belly an' bawl.' This is intensity.

The Bible tells us that it is the effective, fervent prayer of the righteous man that avails much (James 4:16). God is looking for intensity in prayer, not half-hearted, casual prayers. Someone has said that there is a difference to be made between saying prayers and praying. It is certainly neither the length of the prayer that matters, nor the volume. It is not the pious language of the prayer that matters. What always matters to God is the intensity of the prayer.

The Bible promises that those who sow in tears will reap in joy (Psalm 126:5). Notice there will be reaping when there is weeping. Praise God, weeping may endure for the night but joy comes in the morning (Psalm 30: 5). May God give us intensity in our asking so that our prayer life might not become dry, mundane and stale, but will reverberate with passion and power! Where are those who will "weep o'er the erring ones" and "lift up the fallen?" Are you one of those who will make such prayer with sincerity, and with intensity?

The story is told of the single parent, Monica, who had dedicated her son to God as a baby. However, that son grew up to be a rebel. He became a drunkard and he was promiscuous. Although he was exceptionally brilliant intellectually, he used his knowledge against God. His mother was a very devoted woman and she was well known in her community as a godly woman. Because of this she had the opportunity to get a private appointment with a visiting speaker. Her request of the speaker was that he would pray for her son. When the speaker made it clear to her that he did not need to pray for her son she burst into tears asking, "What then is going to happen to my son?" The speaker said to her, "Woman, the son of those tears can never perish," and with that she left his presence even more committed to pray for her son.

Some time after, Monica's son was in his garden relaxing when he heard a voice saying, "Take up and read." At first he dismissed the voice, thinking it was the voice of a child playing nearby. However, when he heard it the third time he knew it was the voice of God telling him to take up the Bible and read. He went inside his house, took up the old Bible and somehow turned to Romans chapter one.

As he read he was convicted of the Holy Spirit and committed his life to Christ. Today, that son is not remembered as Monica's promiscuous son but as Saint Augustine, Bishop of Hippo, North Africa, one of the greatest theologians of the Church.[87]

There is no telling what God will do in response to the intense prayer of a broken heart. "Blessed are those who mourn, for they shall be comforted" (Matthew 5:4). Have we forgotten what it is to weep before God? Tears are a language that God understands. Leonard Ravenhill says:

> When a couple of struggling Salvation Army officers wrote to William Booth telling him they tried every way to get a move and failed, he sent this terse reply, "Try tears." They did. And they had revival.[88]

Charles G. Finney says "There can be no revival when Mr Amen and Mr Wet Eyes are not found in the audience."[89] Again, Ravenhill says concerning intensity in prayer:

> No man is greater than his prayer life. The pastor that is not praying is playing; the people who are not praying are straying...Poverty-stricken as the church is today in many things, she is most stricken here, in the place of prayer. We

> have many organizers, but few agonizers, many players and
> payers, few prayers; many singers, few clingers; lots of pas-
> tors, few wrestlers; many fears, few tears; much fashion,
> little passion; many interferers, few intercessors, many
> writers but few fighters[90]

We certainly need more Christians defined by their passion
for prayer. May God give us a greater passion for prayer, "for he
who dwells in the secret place of the Most High shall abide under
the shadow of the Almighty" (Psalm 91:1). May God give us the
kind of passion that Moses had when he stood before God for his
guilty nation and pleaded for mercy. Moses pleaded with God for
their lives. In fact, he was even willing for God to blot him out of
His book and spare the nation of Israel (Exodus 32:32).

Another biblical character whose life is instructive for us in
regard to prayer is Esther, who risked her life to go into the presence of the king uninvited, so that she could represent her people before the king. The biblical account tells us that through the
wickedness of Haman, a decree was passed to destroy the Jewish
people. Esther sought to approach the king for mercy.

How many of us who are in the Kingdom of God are taking
the time to approach the Mercy Seat, to cry out for those who are
dying in sin and are on their way to a Christless eternity? All of us
who are in the Kingdom must recognize that we are in the Kingdom "for such a time as this" (Esther 4:14).

Daniel was another person who was devoted to prayer. He
prayed three times a day with his window open toward Jerusalem.
Even when the decree was passed that no one should ask anyone for
anything except the king, he was still devoted to prayer. His devo-

tion to prayer led to his deliverance from the lions' den, or more accurately, the den of lions. This was a demonstration to all the people of Persia that there is a God who hears and answers prayer (Daniel 6).

The Bible also tells us that Elijah prayed earnestly that it should not rain and it did not rain for three years and six months. Elijah was a human being just like us, and the God of Elijah is still our God. It is said that American Missionary to Natives Americans David Brainerd knelt in the snow and prayed until it melted around him. That is intensity in prayer.

From 1988 to 1989 we had the joy of hosting a missionary by the name of Brother Gabriel Sharoon at our church at Annotto Bay Gospel Chapel in St. Mary, Jamaica. He is the greatest prayer warrior I have met in the flesh. Sometimes, he would spend seven hours each day in prayer.

Brother Gabriel's life continues to be an example and challenge to me and I thank God for people like him who give themselves to prevailing prayer. I am convinced that the Lord will call some persons to devote their lives to the ministry of intercession. It must neither be considered a ministry for people who have nothing else to do, nor, a ministry of lesser importance. Our Lord Jesus Christ is the supreme example of intercession. Speaking of Jesus, the Bible says:

> 7 who, in the days of His flesh, when He had offered up prayers and supplications, with vehement cries and tears to Him who was able to save Him from death, and was heard because of His godly fear. (Hebrews 5:7)

And in another place: "Therefore He is also able to save to the uttermost those who come to God through Him, since He always lives to make intercession for them" (Hebrews 7:25). I believe we all can identify with Peter, to whom the Lord said:

> "Simon, Simon! Indeed, Satan has asked for you, that he may sift you as wheat. 32 But I have prayed for you, that your faith should not fail; and when you have returned to Me, strengthen your brethren." (Luke 22:31-32).

Had it not been for the prayer of Jesus, where would you be today? I know I would not be here today. It is a glorious thought to know that Jesus, our personal intercessor and Lord, is calling our names to God in prayer.

Prayer is the key to revival. We are aware of it. Yet, we practice so little of it. We need to cry out to God from a prayerful, broken heart. Prayer needs to be our number one pre-occupation. Yet, sometimes we are more preoccupied with action than unction. We are often more concerned about equipment rather than endurment, and we spend more time travelling than travailing. "Prayer is profoundly simple and simply profound."[91]

Prayer, however, has an internal dimension. We must always consider the integrity of the one who prays.

B. He displayed the Integrity of the Asker (verse 3)

Hezekiah passed the integrity test. He was able to say to the Lord, "Remember now, O Lord, I pray, how I have walked before you with truth and with a loyal heart, and have done what was good in your sight" (2 Kings 20:3). How many people can say to the Lord, "Lord I have served you with truth and with a loyal heart?"

Hezekiah was able to say that to God, for he was a man of integrity. It is not only the intensity of the asking that is important when it comes to prayer, but the integrity of the asker. The Bible reminds us that it is the effectual fervent prayer of a righteous man that avails much. The prayer of whom? A righteous man! Many times we are the hindrances to our own prayer, hampered by our iniquities, not God's abilities:

> Behold, the Lord's hand is not shortened, that it cannot save;
> Nor His ear heavy that it cannot hear.
> But your iniquities have separated you from your God;
> And your sins have hidden His face from you (Isaiah 59:1-2).

Sin is always a hindrance to prayer. Someone has said, 'sin will keep us from prayer but prayer will keep us from sin.' God puts the question: Who may ascend into the Hill of the Lord? Or who may stand in His holy place? God also answers the question:

> He who has clean hands and a pure heart,
> Who has not lifted up his soul to an idol
> Nor sworn deceitfully
> He shall receive blessing from the Lord,
> And righteousness from the God of His salvation. (Psalm 24:4-5).

In Psalm 15:1 the question is also asked, "Lord, who may abide in Your tabernacle, Who may dwell in Your holy hill?" Again, the answer comes: "He who walks uprightly, and works righteousness, and speaks the truth in his heart." Do you wish to ascend into the hills of the Lord and dwell in his tabernacle? Then, integrity is important. In 1 Peter 3:12 we are told that, "the eyes of the Lord are on the righteous (italics mine)/, And his ears are open to their prayers; but the face of the Lord is against those who do evil."

The Bible also tells us in Hebrews 5:7 that Jesus' prayer was heard because "he feared" (KJV). The word translated "feared" literally means "piety" or "reverence." It is true that we cannot impress God by our acts of righteousness or piety but it is also true that our sinfulness and lack of reverence will prevent us from drawing close to God as well as hinder our prayer life. Let us consider some specific hindrances to prayer.

1. Selfishness hinders prayer

James 4:3 tells us: "You ask and do not receive, because you ask amiss, that you may spend it on your pleasures". Selfishness hinders prayer. *If you ask amiss your prayer must have been a miss.* By the way, to ask "amiss" means to ask with the wrong motive. Here James was talking about prayers based on selfish pleasures. Prayers with selfish motives are not acceptable unto God.

Yes, Hezekiah prayed prayers of intensity. Yes, he cried out to God for deliverance. But what was his motive? What was his passion? I believe that we can find the secret to all that Hezekiah did in 2 Kings. Here we find the secret of Hezekiah's passion:

"O Lord God of Israel, the One who dwells between the cherubim, You are God, You alone, of all the kingdoms of the earth."

"Now therefore, O Lord our God, I pray, save us from his hand, that all the kingdom of the earth may know that You are the Lord God, You alone"

His passion was for the kingdoms of the earth to come to acknowledge God. Hezekiah was convinced that there is one God who rules the kingdoms of the earth, and he wanted all nations to be confronted with that reality. Hezekiah recognized that God is a global God and so Hezekiah was passionate for the world to know this God.

In the model prayer that the Lord taught His disciples, we find the request for God's Kingdom to come on earth, even as it is in heaven. This request for God's will and purpose to be done on earth should take priority over requests for personal needs. Do you have a passion for the Kingdom of God to be established, as a priority, above your personal needs? Do you desire that the kingdoms of the earth may come to know that God alone is God, even above your own personal comfort or gratification?

Do you have a vision for the 10/40 window—that section of the globe in which the unreached people groups are most concentrated? There, approximately 90 percent of the world's unreached people groups live, yet, less than ten percent of the world's missionaries minister there. There, in that window, less than one percent of the missionary dollar is sent. According to Patrick Johnstone and Jason Mandryk, "the sobering fact is that…probably 15-25% of the world's population has not really heard the gospel in such a way as to respond to the offer of eternal salvation in Jesus Christ."[92]

If we are not concerned about the vast majority of unreached people, then in light of our mandate to make disciples of all nations, I cannot help but conclude that we are selfish. In fact, it is cruel not to share the gospel of Jesus Christ with those who are on their way to a lost eternity. Do you carry a burden for the advancement of the work of the Lord in your local context? Before you pray "give us this day our daily bread," start praying "Thy Kingdom come Thy will be done in earth as is in heaven."

Do you carry a burden for the 2,252 languages that are still without a single verse of Scripture today?[93] Are you concerned about the 3,500 people groups (of all population sizes) that are still not engaged by any Christian missionary outreach?[94] Do you care about the 1.02 billion people in our world that are hungry or the 16,000 children that die each day from hunger related causes (one child dies ever five seconds from hunger)[95] How about stopping right now to consider the welfare of someone less fortunate than you, and lend a helping hand? We cannot afford to centre our prayers on selfish concerns to gratify desires when there are between 100 million and 150 million people living in poverty.[96]

2. Pride hinders prayer

Pride in prayer is evident when we try to be prominent. Praying to be seen by others is related to pride. Praying to be seen by others does not yield any positive result. It carries no heavenly reward. If our motive in prayer is to be seen by men we are being vain and hypocritical. Jesus condemned all prayer for the wrong motive.

And when you pray, you shall not be like the hypocrites.
For they love to pray standing in the synagogues and on
the corners of the streets, that they may be seen by men.
Assuredly I say to you, they have their reward. But you,
when you pray, go into your room, and when you have shut
your door, pray to your Father who is in the secret place;
and your Father who sees in secret will reward you openly
(Matthew 6:5,6).

God knows the integrity of every praying heart. Leonard
Ravenhill said it well when he wrote: "The secret of praying is
praying in secret."[97] If our motivation for prayer is to be seen by
others then that is all the result we will get, and nothing more—to
be seen by people.

3. Stinginess hinders prayer

In the book of Proverbs we read these relevant words: "Whoever, shuts his ears to the cry of the poor Will also cry himself and
not be heard" (Proverbs 21:13). God cannot put anything in our
hands if they are always closed. In the New Testament we are told:

38 Give, and it will be given to you: good measure, pressed
down, shaken together, and running over will be put into
your bosom. For with the same measure that you use, it
will be measured back to you (Luke 6:38).

Good giving requires us to give to God our tithe and offerings. It is dangerous to withhold tithes and offerings. The Bible
tells us that those who withhold tithes and offerings are guilty of
robbing God:

> 8 "Will a man rob God?
> Yet you have robbed Me!
> But you say,
> 'In what way have we robbed You?'
> In tithes and offerings.
> 9 You are cursed with a curse,
> For you have robbed Me,
> Even this whole nation.
> 10 Bring all the tithes into the storehouse,
> That there may be food in My house,
> And try Me now in this,"
> Says the Lord of hosts,
> "If I will not open for you the windows of heaven
> And pour out for you such blessing
> That there will not be room enough to receive it.
> (Malachi 3:8-10)

All who are guilty of robbing God are cheating themselves out of God's blessings. The whole nation of Israel was under a curse because they had robbed God. The Bible says:

> Honour the Lord with your possessions, And with the firstfruits of all your increase; So your barns will be filled with plenty, and your vats will overflow with new wine (Proverbs 3:9-10).

We must give to God what is right, not what is left. If we are faithful in giving to God what is due to Him, He will supply all our needs according to his riches in glory (Philippians 4:19).

4. Unforgiveness hinders prayer

One of the hardest but most necessary things we must do to be effective in praying, is to forgive others.

> Whenever you stand praying, if you have anything against another, forgive him, that your father in heaven may also forgive you your trespasses (Mark 11:25).

Notice that we are required to forgive others if God is to be expected to forgive us. Furthermore, we are exhorted to forgive others as much as Christ has forgiven us (Colossians 3:14). Now, that's a whole lot of forgiveness. Many people cannot sleep because they refuse to forgive others. Some cannot eat, because of unforgiveness. Others suffer physical and psychological health problems because of unforgiveness. Many people cannot pray because of harbouring unforgiveness. There is no alternative. We must forgive.

God is able to deal with the deepest of hurts. We are not wise to cover up hurts, hoping that they will somehow go away. That will not happen. We who are hurting must go to the brother or sister and restore the relationship.

When we behave like that, others will know that we are His disciples. The procedure is necessary for happiness. Asking or extending forgiveness is never easy, therefore, you will have to ask God to give you the grace to love those who have offended you and to apologise to anyone you have offended. If this is done, revival will come. But if such is not done, revival will tarry.

Unforgiveness will always be a roadblock on the path to revival. Selwyn Hughes tells of how a revival broke out in Uganda when one Christian walked more than 100 miles to ask the forgiveness of another Christian, whom he had wronged, twenty years previously.[98]

5. Bad spousal relationships hinder prayer

A wrong relationship between husband and wife is also a hindrance to prayer. The Bible tells us in plain words:

> Husbands, likewise, dwell with them with understanding, giving honour to the wife, as to the weaker vessel, and as being heirs together of the grace of life, that your prayers may not be hindered (1 Peter 2:7)

Those who are seeking God for revival must ensure that their home is in order. Husbands must love their wives, who must respect their husbands.

6. Doubting hinders prayer

God wants us to pray in confidence always, never doubting. Whatever request we make must be made with every assurance God will grant our request. The Bible tells us how we should ask:

> But let him ask…in faith with no doubting, for he who doubts is like a wave of the sea driven and tossed by the wind. For let not that man suppose that he will receive anything from the Lord.

Our prayer for revival, to be effective, must be made in faith in the omnipotent God and His infallible Word. Let us heed the exhortation of Jesus Christ Himself:

"Have faith in God. For assuredly I say to you, whoever says to this mountain, 'Be removed and be cast into the sea,' and does not doubt in his heart, but believes that those things he says will be done, he will have whatever he says. Therefore I say to you, whatever things you ask when you pray, believe that you receive them, and you will have them..." (Mark 11:22b-24)

Faithlessness is a hindrance to effectiveness in prayer but the prayer of faith will move mountains. Only revival prayer will bring revival fire.

Six hindrances have been mentioned, all of which rob our prayer life of vitality. If we do not remove these hindrances from our lives our prayers will go no further than the roof.

May God give us integrity in our hearts that our prayers be not hindered! There is a remedy for sin that has been provided by Jesus Christ and it is His precious blood: "the blood of Jesus Christ His Son cleanses us from all sin" (1 John 1:7). Because Jesus shed his precious blood upon the Cross of Calvary we can have forgiveness of sins. It does not matter how long the sin has been committed or how often it was committed or what kind of sin was committed, the blood of Jesus is still able to remove it. He is a forgiving God.

Anyone who appropriates the blood of Jesus Christ can immediately find complete forgiveness of sin. And God's forgiveness is final: "As far as the east is from the west, *So* far has He removed our transgressions from us" (Psalm 103:12).

There is only one remedy for sin, and it is the blood of Jesus Christ. It is able to deal with all sins that are hindrances to prayer.

Having looked at how Hezekiah demonstrated the intensity of the asking and how Hezekiah displayed the integrity of the asker, let us now look at how Hezekiah discovered the immensity of the Answer. Where there is intensity in prayer, and integrity in the life of those who are asking, the answer will come with immensity.

B. He discovered the immensity of the answer (verses 5-6)

The Bible tells us:

> 4 And it happened, before Isaiah had gone out into the middle court, that the word of the Lord came to him, saying, 5 "Return and tell Hezekiah the leader of My people, 'Thus says the Lord, the God of David your father: "I have heard your prayer, I have seen your tears; surely I will heal you. On the third day you shall go up to the house of the Lord. 6 And I will add to your days fifteen years. I will deliver you and this city from the hand of the king of Assyria; and I will defend this city for My own sake, and for the sake of My servant David." (2 Kings 20:4-6).

The immensity of God's answer is always overwhelming, as Hezekiah discovered. When Hezekiah sent up his cry of *despair*, God sent down the *repair*. God answered immediately. He healed

Hezekiah of his illness. He gave him fifteen more years. He also dealt with Hezekiah's enemies, who had come to destroy Judah. In one night, God solved Hezekiah's problems:

> 35 And it came to pass on a certain night that the angel of the Lord went out, and killed in the camp of the Assyrians one hundred and eighty-five thousand; and when people arose early in the morning, there were the corpses—all dead. 36 So Sennacherib king of Assyria departed and went away, returned home, and remained at Nineveh. 37 Now it came to pass, as he was worshiping in the temple of Nisroch his god that his sons Adrammelech and Sharezer struck him down with the sword; and they escaped into the land of Ararat. Then Esarhaddon his son reigned in his place (2 Kings 19:35-37).

When we consider this answer, the word of the prophet Isaiah comes to mind: "When the enemy comes in like a flood, The Spirit of the Lord will lift up a standard against him" (Isaiah 59:19). God still answers the prayer of intensity and integrity with immensity. God is still able to do more than we can ask or think (Ephesians 3:20). He is still the miracle-working God. He is still able to intervene supernaturally in circumstances that seem impossible. Yes, God is well able to deal with every circumstance that you are facing in your life at this moment.

Remember that He is still the great big wonderful God, who is always victorious and always watching over us. Nothing is too hard for God. There is nothing that can take God by surprise and there is no problem that He cannot solve or issue that He cannot resolve. "Trust in Him at all times, you people; Pour out your heart before Him; God is a refuge for us" (Psalm 62:8). In another place the psalmist says:

> 5 Trust in the Lord with all your heart,
> And lean not on your own understanding;
> 6 In all your ways acknowledge Him,
> And He shall direct your paths.
> (Proverbs 3:5-6)

The Word of the Lord certainly encourages us to approach the throne of grace with boldness and make petition: "Let us therefore come boldly to the throne of grace, that we may obtain mercy and find grace to help in time of need" (Hebrews 4:16). Let us not be afraid to cry out to him now, even if we have to find a solitary place to give Him our undivided attention. We must offer prayers of intensity as we unburden our souls to the Lord. When there is brokenness in the heart, there will be openness in the heavens.[99] How much time are you devoting to fervent prayer? What quality of prayer are you devoting to prayer?

Missions writer C. Peter Wagner once conducted a survey to find out how much time pastors spend in prayer each day.[100] He found that in America 57% of pastors spend 20 minutes daily in prayer, 34% of pastors spend 20 minutes to one hour in daily prayer, and 9 % spend one hour or more in daily prayer.

This research was expanded to include other countries, and it was found that in Australia, pastors spend an average of 23 minutes in daily prayer, in New Zealand pastors spend an average of

30 minutes in daily prayer, in Japan pastors spend 44 minutes in daily prayer, and in Korea pastors spend an average of 90 minutes in daily prayer.

Korea was noted to be the place where the most time was devoted to prayer and the superior results are evident. According to missions researcher Patrick Johnstone, the conversion rate in Korea is greater than the birth rate. He reports that over twenty churches are planted every day in South Korea.[101] Not surprisingly, South Korea has the world's largest single congregation (Full Gospel Central Church) and the largest Presbyterian and Methodist congregations in the world.

Johnstone further points out that South Korea has had the largest evangelistic crusade (by Billy Graham in 1973), the largest Christian Mobilization (in 1974 and 1980 with 2,700,000 attending one meeting), the largest baptismal service since Pentecost (in the Army, which is now 65% Christian), and the largest theological seminaries[102]

The immensity of answer to prayer is also seen in periods of spiritual awakenings. One such awakening took place in Wales with Evans Roberts as one of the major leaders. Evans Roberts himself was just an ordinary coal miner who had a passion for God and prayer. Dr. Bill Bright mentions that Evans Roberts tried to get an opportunity to share his burden at his church, but was refused for quite a while.

However, because of his persistence he was eventually given an opportunity to speak after the Wednesday night meeting, if people would remain to listen to him. A few people stayed to hear what he had to say. Soon, more and more people started staying back. It was not long before a large number of people had caught a burden for passionate prayer that would result in revival.[103] In 1904 that united prayer led to revival in Wales. As Evan Roberts, the coal miner preached, many things happened. Dr. Tangeman gives an account of this revival in his book, The Disciple Making Church:

> Soon the main road on which the church was located was packed solid with hungry seekers coming to the services. Shopkeepers even closed early, so that they too could get a seat in the large but packed church. Christians repented of their sins, and revival spread throughout the countryside. In five months 100,000 people in the immediate area met Christ. Judges had no cases to try. There were no robberies, no burglaries, no rapes, no murders. Civic leaders met to discuss what to do with the police now that crime had disappeared. In one community one police sergeant was asked by a newspaper, "What do you do with your time?"

> "Before the revival," he said, "we had two main jobs; to prevent crimes and to control crowds attending soccer games. Since the revival there is practically no crime. So we just go with the crowds."

> "But how does that affect the police," asked the reporter.

> "We have seventeen police in our station. Five do nothing but control crowds on their way to prayer meetings."

> "What about the other twelve?"

> "Oh, we've organized three quartets with those officers," the sergeant replied.

"They sing at the churches. If any church wants a quartet, they just call the police station."[104]

Similar results were seen in Jamaica in 1860 when the island experienced its only wide scale revival in history. Tony Cauchi had this to say of the Jamaican revival:

> A PHENOMENAL REVIVAL occurred in Jamaica in 1860, ignited by the great North American prayer-revival of 1857-58, which affected a great portion of the Western World.
>
> It was during September 1860, that this unprecedented evangelical awakening began among the Moravians in the parish of St. Elizabeth, in the southwest. It soon spread like wild fire, first to the three parishes of St. James, Hanover, and Westmoreland, causing a sensation in local congregations, regardless of denomination. Eastwards the movement quickened to Mandeville and spread along the coast to villages and hamlets, eventually affecting the entire island—from Montego Bay to St. Thomas, from St. Ann's Bay to Savanna-la-Mar.
>
> The most notable feature of this awakening was prayer. People whose lips seemed solely accustomed to curse and to swear now prayed as fluently as if such petition had been the daily employment of their lives. The prayer meetings seemed to generate a supernatural force which carried the multitudes along on a wave of irresistible power which, in turn, produced passionate repentance, astonishing moral reformation and fervent longing to know and love and serve the Lord Jesus Christ.[105]

With respect to the phenomenal increase in numbers Cauchi reports that

Great crowds were awe-struck. The few scoffers were besieged by the prayers of their friends until they saw the light of the Gospel. Conversions of the most depraved characters were followed by their untiring ministry on behalf of others. New converts by hundreds went from house to house all day and often at night, entreating sinners to repent. Private homes became holy meeting places for public prayer and Bible reading, with 50 or 100 crammed together in each place. Sales of Scriptures from the Kingston depot had averaged 4,700 a year but 20,700 copies were issued during the extraordinary awakening of the years 1860 and 1861.

Convicted sinners were sometimes smitten "deaf and dumb" or gnashed their teeth, or screamed, or tore their clothes. Some were unconscious for a day or more, others speechless for a week or so. It was not "the fear of hell, but a sense of sin" which brought about distress, they said. Often people told of seeing special visions. "Unaccountable" prostrations were sometimes followed by terrific bodily contortions or by jumping, by shouting, and by wild actions.

The Baptists announced more than 6,000 baptised or restored to membership with another 6,000 applying for baptism and fellowship.

So great was the Congregationalist growth that the London Missionary Society, by 1867, considered the field sufficiently evangelised and withdrew its missionaries completely.

The United Presbyterian Church of Scotland announced, "the most remarkable and encouraging (news) that have ever come from Jamaica." Their church membership grew by almost 25 per cent and by the close of 1860 there were 1,928 candidates awaiting admission to membership, and one year later another 1,703.[106]

Let us pray earnestly that God will visit our respective nations with a mighty revival. I am praying and longing for Jamaica to once again experience revival.

The revivals described above are good examples of the immensity of God's answer to prayer. There is nothing too difficult for God to do. That which is impossible for man is possible for God. If you have been praying for the salvation of a relative or friend or even a whole community or people group, do not give up now. God still hears and answers prayer. When God is ready to bless, He often blesses us to overflowing, so that we also can be a blessing to others with overflowing. He is not a stingy God. He blesses with immensity. When he gives us bread, He often gives us with it peanut butter and jelly. Prayers of intensity and integrity will help us to discover God's answers of immensity.

V

HEZEKIAH'S WEAKNESS

He Responded Inappropriately to the Blessings of God

²⁰ Now because of this King Hezekiah and the prophet Isaiah, the son of Amoz, prayed and cried out to heaven. ²¹ Then the Lord sent an angel who cut down every mighty man of valour, leader, and captain in the camp of the king of Assyria. So he returned shamefaced to his own land. And when he had gone into the temple of his god, some of his own offspring struck him down with the sword there. ²² Thus the Lord saved Hezekiah and the inhabitants of Jerusalem from the hand of Sennacherib the king of Assyria, and from the hand of all others, and guided them on every side. ²³ and many brought gifts to the Lord, at Jerusalem, and presents to Hezekiah king of Judah, so that he was exalted in the sight of all nations thereafter.

²⁴ In those days Hezekiah was sick and near death, and he prayed to the Lord; and He spoke to him and gave him a sign. ²⁵ But Hezekiah did not repay according to the favour shown him, for his heart was lifted up; therefore wrath was looming over him and over Judah and Jerusalem. ²⁶ Then Hezekiah humbled himself for the pride of his heart, he and the inhabitants of Jerusalem, so that the wrath of the Lord did not come upon them in the days of Hezekiah.

[27] Hezekiah had very great riches and honour, and he made himself treasuries for silver, for gold, for precious stones, for spices, for shields, and for all kind of desirable items; [28] storehouses for the harvest of grain, wine, and oil; and stall for all kinds of livestock, and folds for flocks. [29] Moreover he provided cities for himself, and possessions of flocks and herds in abundance; for God had given him very much prosperity. [30] This same Hezekiah also stopped the water outlet of Upper Gihon, and brought the water by tunnel to the west side of the City of David. Hezekiah prospered in all his works. [31] However, regarding the ambassadors of the princes of Babylon, whom they sent to him to inquire about the wonder that was done in the land, God withdrew from him, in order to test him, that he might know all that was in his heart (2 Chronicles 32: 20-31)

King Hezekiah *related correctly to God*, *restored God's glory to his nation*, *rebelled against the enemy*, and *resorted to fervent prayer*. All those things set the stage for Judah to experience the mighty intervention of God, who was pleased to intervene miraculously in the lives of His people because of the stance that King Hezekiah took. It was revival time in Judah. The windows of heaven were opened and God was pouring out his blessings—left, right, and centre.

During this revival there was great abundance. God Himself was doing a mighty work among His people, manifesting His presence in no uncertain manner, answering the prayers of Hezekiah and Isaiah, and responding to the renewed quest for His divine intervention in Judah. This is how God works. Whenever people deliberately seek God, He reveals Himself to them. He says: "You will seek Me and find Me, when you search for Me with all your heart" (Jeremiah 29:13). His Word is clear and His promise is true:

If My people who are called by My name will humble themselves, and pray and seek My face, and turn from their
wicked ways, then I will hear from heaven, and will forgive
their sin and heal their land (2 Chronicles 7:14).

Judah was experiencing a time of healing for the land for the
people had humbled themselves and so they were praying and seeking the face of God. They had also turned from their wicked ways.
It was revival time.

However, the story does not end when God answers fervent
prayers. He is interested in how we respond to His mighty acts.
The miracles wrought by God are not ends in themselves. They are
not simply to make us happy and comfortable. They are designed
to engender greater praise and thanksgiving. They should lead us
to love Him more and serve him better. They should lead us to a
closer walk with God. Indeed, they should challenge us to further
commitment. They should help us to know experientially that we
serve a God who hears and answers prayers.

The life of Hezekiah teaches sobering lessons about the
importance of responding correctly to the manifold blessings of
God. We will do well, therefore, to examine more closely what
the Scriptures say in 2 Chronicles 32:20-33, about how to behave
when God is blessing.

The text identified underscores the magnitude of the blessing God lavished on King Hezekiah and the inhabitants of Judah
during a period of great revival. What God did for Hezekiah and
his people was spectacular, magnificent, supernatural and extraordinary. God's working was clearly miraculous. While it is true
that God is always at work in this universe and in our lives and circumstances, it is also true that there are times when God chooses

to suspend the natural order of things and intervene supernaturally, for a purpose. Let us consider the magnitude of the blessings that Hezekiah experienced, and God's special intervening work.

A. He experienced the magnitude of blessing (verses 20-24, 27-31)

God fought Hezekiah's battle for him. When we trust God no enemy can stand before us. The Word of God tells us that

> ...the Lord sent an angel who cut down every mighty man of valour, leader and captain in the camp of the king of Assyria. So he returned shame faced to his own land (2 Chronicles 32:21)

The king of Assyria was a mighty man with a mighty army, but as the same verse tells us, while he was in the temple of his god, "some of his own offspring struck him down with the sword." We see, therefore, how God supernaturally *destroyed* the enemy and *demolished* his plan. The word used to describe what God did to the enemies in 2 Chronicles 32:21 is *bakar,* which means "to cut off, or demolish, to make to disappear."[107] From 2 Kings 19:35 we learn that the total number in the enemy's camp that was destroyed in that incident was 185,000.

It is still God's intention to destroy the Devil and demolish his wicked plans. God's Word tells us that it is for this purpose "the Son of God was manifested, that he might destroy the works of the devil"(1 John 3:8). Jesus died so that "through His death he might destroy him who had the power of death, that is, the devil" (Hebrew 2:14).

Even as God destroyed Hezekiah's enemies and demolished his plans, so He will demolish every plan of the Enemy that is arrayed against us—our families, our ministries, and our nation. If we pray fervently and serve God faithfully, no weapon that is formed against us shall prosper (Isaiah 54:17). David rejoices with assurance in the goodness and greatness of God on our behalf. He says:

1 The Lord is my light and my salvation;
Whom shall I fear?
The Lord is the strength of my life;
Of whom shall I be afraid?
2 When the wicked came against me
To eat up my flesh,
My enemies and foes,
They stumbled and fell.
3 Though an army may encamp against me,
My heart shall not fear;
Though war may rise against me,
In this I will be confident.
4 One thing I have desired of the Lord,
That will I seek:
That I may dwell in the house of the Lord
All the days of my life,
To behold the beauty of the Lord,
And to inquire in His temple.
5 For in the time of trouble
He shall hide me in His pavilion;
In the secret place of His tabernacle
He shall hide me;
He shall set me high upon a rock.
Wait, I say, on the Lord!
(Psalm 27:1-5)

How comforting and wonderful to know for sure that God Himself will take care of the forces of darkness that fight against us. Our hearts can be knit with that of the psalmist who prophetically reminds us:

1 He who dwells in the secret place of the Most High
Shall abide under the shadow of the Almighty.
2 I will say of the Lord, "He is my refuge and my fortress;
My God, in Him I will trust."
3 Surely He shall deliver you from the snare of the fowler
And from the perilous pestilence.
4 He shall cover you with His feathers,
And under His wings you shall take refuge;
His truth shall be your shield and buckler.
5 You shall not be afraid of the terror by night,
Nor of the arrow that flies by day,
6 Nor of the pestilence that walks in darkness,
Nor of the destruction that lays waste at noonday.
7 A thousand may fall at your side,
And ten thousand at your right hand;
But it shall not come near you.
8 Only with your eyes shall you look,
And see the reward of the wicked.
9 Because you have made the Lord, who is my refuge,
Even the Most High, your dwelling place,
10 No evil shall befall you,
Nor shall any plague come near your dwelling;
11 For He shall give His angels charge over you,
To keep you in all your ways.
12 In their hands they shall bear you up,
Lest you dash your foot against a stone.
(Psalm 91:1-12)

The Lord is quite able, and He is also willing to destroy every Enemy that comes against us, and to demolish the enemy's every plan. We do not have to fear the destructive plans of the enemy, as long as the blood of Jesus is upon us. His blood avails and His blood prevails.

Not only did God *destroy* Hezekiah's enemies and *demolished* their plans, but he also *delivered* Hezekiah from their hands:

> The Lord saved Hezekiah and the inhabitants of Jerusalem from the hand of Sennacherib the king of Assyria, and from the hand of all others (2 Chronicles 32:22)

The word *yasa,* which is translated 'saved' here, also means 'deliver.' It means "to save, implying in the largest sense, deliverance, help, and victory"[108] The word refers to either the "removal of evil and misery or the restoration of good and former happiness"[109] It is the same word used for the spiritual deliverance that Messiah effected when He paid the price of our redemption.

God delivered Hezekiah from the enemies. He also delivered him from physical illness. He was literally at the point of death when God gave him fifteen more years to live (verse 24. See also 2 Kings 20:1-6). What a great deliverance! What a magnitude of blessing!

The same God who delivered Hezekiah is able to deliver us for He is our rock, our fortress, and our deliverer. We can trust in Him. David said, "This poor man cried, and the Lord heard him, and saved him out of all his trouble" (Psalm 34:6). When we are under oppression and cry unto God, He will hear and answer. The

Children of Israel cried out to God as a result of the oppression and affliction the Egyptians had them under, and God heard and answered:

> 7 And the Lord said: "I have surely seen the oppression of
> My people who are in Egypt, and have heard their cry be-
> cause of their taskmasters, for I know their sorrows. 8 So
> I have come down to deliver them out of the hand of the
> Egyptians, and to bring them up from that land to a good
> and large land, to a land flowing with milk and honey, to
> the place of the Canaanites and the Hittites and the Amori-
> tes and the Perizzites and the Hivites and the Jebusites.

Through a series of miracles the Lord delivered the Children of Israel from the *hand* of the Egyptians—and the *land* of the Egyptians—from the hand and from the land—complete deliverance. That's how God works.

Shadrach, Meshech and Abednego did not bow down to the graven image Nebucadnezzar had set up because they were convinced that the God whom they served was able "to deliver" them. Hear the words of the three Hebrew boys to the King of Babylon:

> If that is the case, our God whom we serve is able to deliver
> us from the burning fiery furnace, and He will deliver us
> from your hand, O king (Daniel 3:17).

Those words of holy boldness were spoken after the king had made it clear to them that if they refused to worship the graven image that he had set up, he would have them cast into the fiery furnace

Now if you are ready at the time you hear the sound of the horn, flute, harp, lyre, and psaltery, in symphony with all kinds of music, and you fall down and worship the image which I have made, good! But if you do not worship, you shall be cast immediately into the midst of a burning fiery furnace. And who is the god who will deliver you from my hands? (Daniel 3:15).

King Nebuchadnezzar in his ignorance and arrogance had challenged the God of the universe. His challenge was in the form of a question, "and who is the God who will deliver you from my hand?" Soon Nebuchadnezzar was able to answer his own question:

Blessed be the God of Shadrach, Meshach, and Abed-Nego, who sent His Angel and delivered His servants who trusted in Him.

The heathen king had to change his words because he witnessed the mighty deliverance of the three Hebrew boys. When they were cast into the fire, a "Fourth Man," described as One like unto the Son of Man, was there with them, in the midst of the burning fiery furnace heated seven times hotter. Yet, praise God, not even the hair on their skin was scorched. Our God is a mighty deliverer!

Also, God miraculously delivered Daniel out of the mouth of lions in such a dramatic way that King Darius was astonished. His question reflects both respect and nervousness:

"Daniel, servant of the living God, has your God, whom you serve continually, been able to deliver you from the lions?" (Daniel 6:20).

Yes, Daniel's God surely delivered, and Daniel's God surely will deliver. "Surely He shall deliver you from the snare of the fowler/ And from the noisome pestilence" (Psalm 91:3).

The magnitude of God's blessing was evident when He destroyed the enemies and demolished their plans. That magnitude was also seen in how God delivered Hezekiah from the hands of the Devil as well as from illness. The magnitude of God's blessing was also seen when He "guided them on every side." In other words, God directed them. To be *directed* by God is indeed a tremendous blessing.

The Hebrew word translated "guided" in this passage, *nahal*, means, "to lead, guide gently, softly and with care, as a shepherd guides his flocks"[110] That is a good description of how God guides. We all have much to give God thanks for when we reflect and recall how God has guided us this far in life. Indeed, when we do so honestly we aught to celebrate His guidance, sharing the sentiments of Joseph Gilmore:

> He leadeth me! O blessed thought!
> O words with heav'ly comfort fraught!
> Whate'er I do, where'er I be,
> Still 'tis God's hand that leadeth me.
>
> Sometimes 'mid scenes of deepest gloom,
> Sometimes where Eden's bower bloom,
> By waters still, o'er troubled sea,
> Still 'tis His hand that leadeth me.[111]

What a tremendous blessing to be directed by the hand of Almighty God! He led the children of Israel through the wilderness for forty years. His presence constantly and consistently directed them through difficult and unfamiliar paths. The account of His leading Israel in the wilderness is truly remarkable:

> The Lord went before them by day in a pillar of cloud to lead the way, and by night in a pillar of fire to give them light, so as to go by day and night. He did not take away the pillar of cloud by day or the pillar of fire by night from before the people (Exodus 13:21-22).

God's leading is always needed. This is because we are all like sheep, prone to go astray. Therefore, we continually need the Lord's direction in our lives. The psalmist David knew what it was to be led by the Lord, and spoke about it with joy in his heart:

> 2 He makes me to lie down in green pastures;
> He leads me beside the still waters.
> 3 He restores my soul;
> He leads me in the paths of righteousness
> For His name's sake.
> (Psalm 23:2-3)

The famous hymn-writer Fanny Crosby expressed the same thought in the words of this song:

> All the way my Savior leads me;
> What have I to ask beside?
> Can I doubt His tender mercy,
> Who thro' life has been my guide?
> heav'nly peace divinest comfort,
> Here by faith in Him to dwell!
> For I know whate'er befall me,
> Jesus doeth all things well;

For I know whate'er befall me,
Jesus doeth all things well;
All the way my Savior leads me;
Cheers each winding path I tread,
Gives me grace for ev'ry trial,
Feeds me with the living bread;
Tho' my weary steps may falter,
and my soul athirst may be,
Gushing from the Rock before me,
Lo! a spring of joy I see;
Gushing from the Rock before me,
Lo! a spring of joy I see;

All the way, my Savior leads me;
Oh, the fullness of His love!
Perfect rest to me is promised
In my Father's house above:
When my spirit, clothed immortal,
Wings its flight to realms of day,
This my song thro' endless ages:
Jesus led me all the way;
This my song thro' endless ages:
Jesus led me all the way;[112]

We have to bow in thanksgiving to God as we remember where he has brought us from, where He has led us to, and how he has directed us through the difficult moments of our lives. Indeed, the magnitude of God's blessing was also seen in how God directed Hezekiah.

Also, God *distinguished* Hezekiah in the sight of all the nations. God made Hezekiah to be "exalted in the sight of all nations" (verse 23). To speak colloquially, God chose to "big up" Hezekiah.

God blessed Hezekiah so much that people began to look up to him. Hezekiah became a man of high esteem, both nationally and internationally. The global community began showering Hezekiah with honour and praise.

When God is ready to promote you, no one can stop it. Because of the mighty work of God in Hezekiah's life and reign, he was thrust into the international spotlight. The news of the mighty acts of God propelled Hezekiah to become an international figure. Leaders of other nations began bringing presents to him (verse 22). When the Lord chooses to lift us up, it is our duty to give Him praise and adoration for, "to whom much is given much is expected" (Luke 12:48).

When God puts us in the limelight our responsibility increases instantly. Yes, our responsibility increases with each new blessing, and privilege. And, with added responsibility comes greater accountability. The wise King Solomon has a word of caution for us in times of praises. He says: "The crucible for silver and the furnace for gold, but man is tested by the praises he receives" (Proverbs 27:21).

God began blessing Judah tremendously. It was a time of success. It was a time of peace and prosperity. It was a time of much publicity. It was a time of abundance. Verses 27-31 tell us of the riches that Hezekiah had and how he had to expand his storehouses to accommodate his possessions. It was a time of great blessing. O the magnitude of blessing! It was a time of refreshing. It was revival time.

But, it was also a time of testing. The interesting statement is made: "God withdrew from him, in order to test him, that he might know all that was in his heart" (verse 31). God will test you on every blessing and privilege that he has given to you. We must constantly remember, especially in the times of success, that we are only stewards of His manifold blessings.

God blessed Hezekiah by *destroying the enemies* and *delivering him* from both the attacks of the enemy and sickness. He blessed him by *directing him* and he blessed him by *distinguishing him* in the eyes of many nations. But how did Hezekiah respond to the magnitude of God's blessing? That is the critical question.

One would have thought that King Hezekiah would have served God with humility and give Him all the glory, seeing that God had spared his life and blessed him tremendously. However, Instead of demonstrating humility in the face of the *magnitude of the blessing* he developed *an attitude of bragging*. Let us now consider his attitude of bragging.

B. He exhibited an attitude of bragging (verse 25)

How sad is it to read: "Hezekiah rendered not again according to the benefit done to him; for his heart was lifted up" (2 Chronicles 32:25). What a disappointing response to the mighty blessings of God! Yet, it is true that in the face of God's blessings many of us adopt an attitude of bragging; an air of self-sufficiency, boasting and indifference to the part God played. Hezekiah did not lack *fortitude* in the face of opposition but he lacked an *attitude of gratitude* in his moments of blessings.

Instead of giving God the glory Hezekiah took it for himself. He got carried away with his successes, although they were not wrought by his own skills and ingenuity. His success was the direct intervention of God. Yet he seemed to have quickly forgotten that very important fact. It is so easy to be swept away by the applause of men in the time of victory. Many people have been brought to ruin by their own successes and accomplishments.

Therefore, sometimes, when God withholds His blessings from us, it is an act of mercy, for many people are not mature enough to deal with great successes. God knows those Christians would backslide instantly, if He were to grant them their heart's desires. Many persons are not prepared enough to have their prayers answered immediately. They are not mature enough to handle the positive answers to their prayer.

It is interesting to note that Hezekiah did not fail the Lord when he was facing hardships. Yet, he stumbled in a time of success and victory. He failed the Lord when he was thrust into the limelight and enjoying *peace, prosperity* and *presents* from the international community. It was not the lust of the flesh, nor the lust of the eyes that caused Hezekiah to stumble, but it was the pride of life. The Bible says: "Pride goes before destruction/ And a haughty spirit before a fall" (Proverbs 16:18). The Bible also reminds us that God resists the proud but gives grace to the humble (James 4:6, 1 Peter 5:5). God's grace is undeserved or unmerited favour. If we humble ourselves before God, He promises to exalt us (1 Peter 5:7). But if we lift up ourselves in pride, He will debase us (Matthew 23:12, Luke 14:11, Luke 18:14).

The sin of pride is a serious offence in the sight of God. A braggadocio attitude is not welcome in the presence of the holy God. It was the sin of pride that caused Satan to be kicked out of heaven. It was the sin of pride, evident in ingratitude, that caused God to forcefully remove King Nebucadnezzar from his throne and thrust him out in the fields to eat grass like an animal (Daniel 4:31-37). It was the sin of pride that caused King Herod to be killed instantly when he refused to give God the glory due to Him:

> Then immediately an angel of the Lord struck him, because he did not give glory to God. And he was eaten by worms and died (Acts 12:23).

It is a dangerous thing to withhold the glory that is due to the Lord.

Even before the Children of Israel entered the Promised Land the Lord warned them of the dangers of forgetting the goodness of God. Failure to remember and celebrate the goodness of God deliberately courts judgement:

> 11 "Beware that you do not forget the Lord your God by not keeping His commandments, His judgments, and His statutes which I command you today, 12 lest—when you have eaten and are full, and have built beautiful houses and dwell in them; 13 and when your herds and your flocks multiply, and your silver and your gold are multiplied, and all that you have is multiplied; 14 when your heart is lifted

up, and you forget the Lord your God who brought you out of the land of Egypt, from the house of bondage; 15 who led you through that great and terrible wilderness, in which were fiery serpents and scorpions and thirsty land where there was no water; who brought water for you out of the flinty rock; 16 who fed you in the wilderness with manna, which your fathers did not know, that He might humble you and that He might test you, to do you good in the end—17 then you say in your heart, 'My power and the might of my hand have gained me this wealth.'

18 "And you shall remember the Lord your God, for it is He who gives you power to get wealth, that He may establish His covenant which He swore to your fathers, as it is this day. 19 Then it shall be, if you by any means forget the Lord your God, and follow other gods, and serve them and worship them, I testify against you this day that you shall surely perish. 20 As the nations which the Lord destroys before you, so you shall perish, because you would not be obedient to the voice of the Lord your God (Deuteronomy 8:11-20).

We are under divine obligation to give God the glory for the many blessings that He has lavished upon us. There is no place to become proud and conceited when God opens His hands to us. The Bible tells us that divine blessings should lead us to repentance (Romans 2:4). If God's blessings do not bring us to repentance, then judgement will.

Instead of becoming a braggart, the blessing of God should lead us into deeper praise and worship. In your time of success, promotion, victory and accomplishments, please remember that they are brought to you by the goodness of God. Don't become proud and conceited because of God's grace and mercy. God is a jealous God and He will not share His glory with anyone.

Perhaps it would be good to pause right now to remember where God has brought you from, and fall down now before Him in worship, praise and adoration. You cannot afford to be indifferent to the part the Almighty God has played in bringing you to this point in life. Reflect on the fact that you didn't get here by your own genius or skill. It is God who enabled you, all the way. When we think of the current blessings the Lord is allowing us to enjoy we do well to reflect on these beautiful words of the hymn-writer Dottie Rambo:

> The things that I love and hold dear to my heart
> Are just borrowed, they're not mine at all;
> Jesus only let me use them to brighten my life,
> So remind me, remind me dear Lord.

> *Roll back the curtain of mem'ry now and then,*
> *Show me where you brought me from and*
> *where I could have been;*
> *Remember I'm human, and humans forget-*
> *So remind me, remind me dear Lord.*

> Nothing good have I done to deserve God's own Son,
> I'm not worthy of the scars in His hands;
> Yet He chose the road to Calv'ry to die in my stead-
> Why He loved me I can't understand.[113]

These words ought to inspire us to go back to Bethel, like Jacob. Jacob was told to go back to Bethel and build an altar to the Lord, for it was there that God met Him when He was fleeing from his brother Esau. He had nothing then but the clothes on his back. His life was at stake. He was down on his face. He was a fugitive and a vagabond. But, in that state, God met him and ministered to him, and he made a vow to God. Many years later, when God met him again, he had great possessions, several wives and children. He was indeed blessed of God. In this experience of great abundance he was told to go back to Bethel, which means 'House of God,' and there build an altar to the Lord (Geneses 35:1).

What are some of the blessings God has bestowed upon you? Recall them and then go back to Bethel and build an altar to the Lord. Don't become a braggart because of God's blessings. When God blesses us, thanksgiving must follow, not bragging. God's blessing must evoke constant streams of praise from our heart and lips:

> O come, let us sing unto the Lord; Let us make a joyful noise to the rock of our salvation. Let us come before his presence with thanksgiving, and make a joyful noise unto him with psalms (Psalm 95:1-2).

When our hearts are full of praise for God, our lips will sing His praises. The Apostle James tells us that then we will sing psalms (James 5:14). The heart inclined to praise, the Apostle Paul tells, will give thanks in everything for this is the will of God (1 Thessalonians 5:18). Therefore, do not be like the nine out of ten lepers who did not return to thank Jesus after He healed them (Luke 17:11-18). Unthankfulness is one of the sins that describes the perilous times of the last days (2 Timothy 3:2). We cannot afford to adopt an attitude of bragging like Hezekiah. Instead, we must remember to render to God according to the blessings that he has bestowed on us.

It is only reasonable for us to show appreciation to God for His many blessings. Hezekiah had done many great things for God, which we can emulate. His life and ministry led to a great renewal in the nation of Judah. However, he had weaknesses. His major weakness was that he did not render to God according to magnitude to the blessings that He lavished on him.

Because of this, he evoked the wrath of God. Because Hezekiah failed to respond appropriately to the mighty intervention of Almighty God in his life and circumstances, he had to pay dearly. His chastisement was made greater because his blessings had been so great. I call this the amplitude of his beating.

C. He encountered the amplitude of the beating (verse 25)

Having looked at the magnitude of the blessing, and the attitude of the bragging, let us now look at the amplitude of the beating, which Hezekiah encountered as a result of his inappropriate response to God's blessings. The Bible tells us that because Hezekiah did not render to God according to the blessings that he enjoyed, there was wrath upon him and Jerusalem. God was greatly displeased with the posture that Hezekiah took and so God's wrath came upon Hezekiah as well as upon the whole nation. Pride and unthankfulness invite the wrath of God.

The Bible tells us that to whom much is given much is expected (Luke 12:48). If we disregard God after he has clearly revealed His will to us and has blessed us greatly, He is going to chastise us greatly. The Bible tells us, "the servant who knew his master's will, and did not prepare himself or do according to his will, shall be beaten with many stripes" (Luke 12:47). God holds us accountable to Him for the knowledge, experiences and blessings that he has given to us. The greater the blessing, the greater chastisement will be if we do not respond appropriately. No wonder the Bible tells us that teachers will be judged with harsher judgment (James 3:1). We must respond appropriately to the blessings of God or face dire consequences.

It seems harsh that God did not allow Moses to enter the Promised Land because he struck the rock to get water when the Lord instructed him to speak to the rock. This was after Moses had done a great work in leading the Children of Israel out of Egyptian captivity. God had chosen to reveal himself to Moses in no uncertain manner. Moses had a knowledge of God that few human beings were privileged to have. We can begin to understand God's seemingly harsh response to Moses when we realise that Moses had an intimacy with God that few, if any other, human being ever had or will have.

King Saul was rejected by God and removed from his throne because of his disobedience to the Word of God. God had elevated Saul to be the first king of Israel. That was a very prestigious position. But, that position also brought with it awesome responsibility. Those whom God has lifted up to serve him must be meticulous, even scrupulous, in their observation of the commands of God.

Someone has rightly pointed out that when a pocket watch goes wrong only one person is misled. But, whenever the town clock goes wrong, the whole city is misled. Therefore, those whom God lifts up to a place of influence must recognize that it is a place of fear and trembling. It must not for even one moment be taken lightly.

When God has used us to be a blessing to His people we must humble ourselves before Him. When God has used us to lead His people into revival we must be careful to give Him glory. We must not touch the glory and take it for ourselves. Glory belongs to God alone. Remember that when the Ark of the Covenant was falling Uzzah put forth his hand to stabilize the Ark of God and fell dead. Uzzah died because he did not treat the Lord's presence with the proper protocol. When the Lord chooses to grace us with His manifest presence, we must be careful to treat such presence with reverence. When God does a mighty work among us, and through us, we must let Him have the pre-eminence. We, the human instruments, must remain humble. In this regard, it is good to heed the message of Micah:

> He has shown you, O man, what *is* good;
> And what does the Lord require of you
> But to do justly,
> To love mercy,
> And to walk humbly with your God?
> (Micah 6:8)

The Apostle Paul in 1 Corinthians warns us: "Wherefore, let him that thinks he stands take heed lest he fall." May God help us to remain standing in the times of adversity as well as in the times of prosperity. It is very easy to fall while the blessings are falling.

Hezekiah experienced the wrath of God because of his sin of pride. Are you experiencing the wrath of God in your life and circumstances because of pride, manifested in unthankfulness? Have you been unfaithful to God in spite of His great blessings? If so, there is still hope. After Hezekiah experienced the wrath of God he humbled himself and once again experienced the mercy of God.

Today, if you will humble yourself before God He will still have mercy on you. He is a God who will abundantly pardon (Isaiah 55:7). Make a fresh commitment to let your life bring glory to God in every way. Consciously give Him praise and glory for all that He has done for you. Like the psalmist, consider the question: "What shall I render to the Lord For all His benefits toward me." (Psalm 116:12). The appropriate response seems pronounced in another psalm:

> 1 Bless the Lord, O my soul;
> And all that is within me, *bless* His holy name!
> 2 Bless the Lord, O my soul,
> And forget not all His benefits:
> 3 Who forgives all your iniquities,
> Who heals all your diseases,
> 4 Who redeems your life from destruction,
> Who crowns you with loving kindness and tender mercies,
> (Psalm 103:1-4)

How wonderful are the tender mercies of God! We are constrained to show our appreciation to God. The Holy Spirit urges us to perform specific acts of service to show our appreciation to God. The Spirit impels us to "give unto the Lord the glory due to his name" (Psalm 29:2) so that we might not experience the tragedy that King Hezekiah did, and which Hezekiah's great grandfather experienced, King Uzziah. The Biblical account says of Uzziah, "his heart was lifted up, to his own destruction" *(*2 Chronicles 26). The Bible tells us, "whoever exalts himself will be humbled, and he who humbles himself will be exalted" (Luke 14:11).

You don't have to try to project yourself and boast about what you have done, or about what you are currently doing, or about what you have achieved or acquired in life. Humble yourself, and leave the rest to God. When you leave things to God you will see that He has a strange way of working, but ultimately, a better way. *Stay humble or you will stumble, if not totally crumble.* When we experience the magnitude of God's blessings let us refuse to exhibit an attitude of bragging, for such leads to the amplitude of beating. Eschew the beating and embrace the blessing. It is revival time.

NOTES

PREFACE

1   Walter Kaiser, Jr. *Quest for Renewal: Personal Revival in the Old Testament.* (Chicago: Moody Press, 1986), p. 13

2   Bill Bright, *The Transforming Power of Fasting and Prayer* (New-Life Publications: Orlando, Florida, 1997), p. 7

3   Richard Bowie, *Light for the Nations (A Biblical Theology of Evangelisation)* (Haggai Centre for Leadership Studies: Tanglin, Singapore, 1992, 1993), p. 83

4   "God is Here," in *Redemption Songs* (London: Pickering & Inglis) No. 6

INRODUCTION

5   *Britannica Online Encyclopedia*, "Postmodernism (philosophy)" http://www.britannica.com/EBchecked/topic/1077292/postmodernism

6   Selwyn Hughes, *Revival: Times of Refreshing* (Lottbridge Drove: Kingsway Publications, 1984), p. 51

7   Grace Online Library, "What is Revival," http://www.graceonlinelibrary.org/articles/full.asp?id=27|28|166 (accessed September 12, 2010)

8   Christ Community Church, "Marks of Revival," http://ccc138.org/article.asp?ID=332 (accessed September 12, 2010)

9   Manny Hooper, *The Effect of Revivals on the World Missionary Movement*.(California: Fuller Theological Seminary, 1987), p. 4

10   J.M. Sinclair, "revival" in *Collins Concise Dictionary*, 5th Ed.

11   Charles Pfeiffer, Howard Vos and John Rea (eds.). *Wycliffe Bible Encyclopaedia* (Chicago: Moody Press, 1975) S.v. "Hezekiah"

12   Tommy Tenny, *The God Chasers* (Shippensburg, Pennsylvania: Destiny Image Publications, 2000), p. 37

13   Charles Pfeiffer and Howard Vos and John Ra (eds.) *Wycliffe Bible Encyclopaedia*, p. 729

14   Ibid, p. 729

15   Robert Coleman, *The Master Plan of Discipleship* (Grand Rapids: Fleming H. Revell, 1987,1988), p. 13

16   J. Edwin Orr, "Cleanse Me" in Praise! *Our Songs and Hymns* (Grand Rapids, Michigan: Singspiration, 1979).

CHAPTER ONE
Hezekiah's Walk: He Related Correctly to God

17   Kenneth Baker (ed.), *The NIV Study Bible*, (Colorado Springs, Colorado: International Bible Society, 1978,1983), p. 559 (Reference notes on 2 Kings 18:3)

18   Ibid, p. 559 (Reference Notes to 2 Kings 18:3)

19   Tommy Tenny, *The Daily Chase* (Shippensburg, Pennsylvania: Destiny Image Publications, 2000), p. 8

20   Ibid, p. v

21   Robert J. Morgan, *Nelson's Complete Book of Stories, Illustrations and Quotes* (Nashville, Tennessee: Thomas Nelson Publishers, 2000), p. 142

22   William Wilson, *Old Testament Word Studies* (Grand Rapids, Michigan: Kregel Publications, 1978) p. 356

23   Neil Anderson, *Setting Your Church Free: A Biblical Plan to Help Your Church* (Ventura, California: Regal Books, 1994), p. 196

24   David Dockery (ed.), *The Challenge of Postmodernism: An Evangelical Engagement* (Wheaton, Illinois: Victor Books, 1995) p. 101

25   Ajith Fernando, *Sharing the Truth in Love: How to Relate to People of Other Faiths* (Grand Rapids, Michigan: Discovery House Publishers, 2001) p. 15

26   Ibid, p. 57

27   Mark Bubeck, *The Adversary: The Christian Versus Demonic Activity*, (Chicago: Moody Press, 1975), p. 30

28   Rick Richardson, *Evangelism Outside the Box: New Ways to Help People Experience the Good News*, (Downers Grove, Illinois: InterVarsity Press, 2000), p. 126

29   Ibid, p.126

30   Tommy Tenny, *The Daily Chase* p., 8

31   David Dockery (ed.), p. 13

32   Aubrey Malphurs, *Advanced Strategic Planning: A New Model For Church and Ministry Leaders* (Grand Rapids, Michigan: Baker Book House, 1999) p. 55

33   Ibid, p. 56

34   Eddie Gibbs and Ian Cofey, *Church Next*, (Downers Grove: Inter-Varsity Press, 2000) p. 146

35   Ajith Fernando, p. 56

36   Ashley Smith, *Emergence from Innocence: Religion, Theology and Development* (Mandeville: Eureka Press, 1991), p. 14

37   Robert Morgan, p. 565

38   Ibid, p. 564

39   Ibid p. 565

40   Henry Blackaby and Claud King, *Experiencing God: Doing and Knowing the Will of God*. (Nashville, Tennessee: LifeWay Press, 1990) p. 112

41   Ibid, p. 113

42   William Wilson, p. 79

43   Johnson Oatman, "Higher Ground" in Praise!: *Our Sons and Hymns*. (Grand Rapids, Michigan: Singspiration, 1979) p., 380

CHAPTER TWO
Hezekiah's Worship: He Retored God's Glory to Judah

44   Robert Morgan, p. 142

45   Evangelical Training Association, *Growing Towards Spiritual Maturity*, (Wheaton, Illinois: Evangelical Training Association, 1998), p.50

46   Arthur Katz, *Apostolic Foundations: The Challenge of Living an Authentic Christian Life* (Minnesota: Burning Bush Publications, 1999), p. 15

47   Blackaby and King, p. 118

48   David Dockery, p. 23

49   Rick Richardson, *Evangelism Outside the Box* (Illinois: Inter-Varsity Press, 2000), p. 51

50   Rick Richardson, p. 51

51   Ibid, p. 106

52   Tommy Tenny, *The God Chasers*, p.37

53   Ibid, p. 37

54   Ralph Carmichael, "The Saviour is Waiting," c 1958 Sacred Songs (a division of Word, Inc) in Praise! Our Songs and Hymns Grand Rapids, Michigan: Sinspiration, 1979), p. 300

55   Arthur Katz, p. 37

56   Ibid, p. 37

57   William Cowper, "There is a fountain Filled With Blood" in *Praise! Our Songs and Hymns* (Grand Rapids, Michigan: Singspiration, 1979), p. 265

58   Selwyn Hughes, p. 36

CHAPTER THREE
Hezekiah's Warfare I:He Rebelled Against the King of Assyria

59 William LaSor, David Hubbard and Frederic Bush, *Old Testament Survey* (Grand Rapids, Michigan: William B. Eerdmans Publishing Company, 1982), p. 278

60 Charles Pfeiffer, Howard Vos and John Rea (eds.) *Wycliffe Bible Encyclopaedia*, S.v. "Hezekiah."

61 George Verwer, *Out of the Comfort Zone*, (Cumbria, OM Publishing, 2000), p. 31

62 Ibid, p. 31

63 Ravnhill, p. 39

64 Mark Bubeck, *Overcoming the Adversary: Warfare Praying Against Demonic Activity*, p. 15

65 Carman, "Revive us O Lord," on Audio Cassette Carman— the Absolute Best. Copyright The Sparrow Corporation, 1993.

66 David and Pat Alexander, *The Lion Handbook of the Bible*, (Hertz: Lion Publishing, 1993), p. 280

67   Madeline S and J Lane Miller. *Harper Encyclopaedia of Bible Life*, ed. Boyce M. Bennett, Jr. and David H. Scott, (Harper and Rowe Publishers, 1978) p. 269

68   John Mallison, *Mentoring to Develop Leaders and Disciples* (Lidcombe: Scripture Union, 1998), p. 34

69   Charles Pfeiffer, Howard Vos and John Rea *Wycliffe Bible Encyclopaedia*, S.v. "Hezekiah."

70   Mark Bubeck, *Overcoming the Adversary*, p. 15

71   This true story was related to a group of us by Emmanuel Richardson at a Christian Brethren Easter Convention Retreat, Silver Palms Villas, November 2000

72   George Duffield, "Sand Up for Jesus," in Praise! *Our Songs and Hymns* (Grand Rapids, Michigan: Singspiration, 1979), p. 456

73   C. Peter Wagner, *Prayer Shield* (Ventura, California: Real Books, 1997), p.48-49

74   W.E. Vine, Merrill Unger and William White, *Vine's Complete Expository Dictionary of Old and New Testament Words*, (Nashville, Tennessee: Thomas Nelson Publishers, 1985), S.v. "Lord"

75   Charles Pfeiffer, Howard Vos and John Rea. *Wycliffe Bible Encyclopaedia*, S.v. "Name(s)"

CHAPTER FOUR
Hezekiah's Warfare II: He Resorted to Fervent Prayers

76 Frank Damazio, *Seasons of Refreshing: Understanding the Appointed Times of Spiritual Refreshing*, (Oregon: Bible Temple Publishing, 1996) p. 363

77 Ibid, p. 364

78 William Taylor, *Global Missiology for the Twenty First Century* (Grand Rapids, Michigan: Baker Book House, 2000), p. 8

79 Jim Cymbala, *Fresh Wind, Fresh Fire* (Grand Rapids, Michigan: Zondervan Publishing House, 1997) p. 58

80 Joseph Scriven, "What a Friend we have in Jesus" in *Praise! Our Songs and Hymns* (Grand Rapids, Michigan: Singspiration, 1979), p. 412

81 Jim Cymbala p. 71

82 Tom White, *Breaking Strongholds: How Spiritual Warfare Sets Captives Free* (Ann Arbor, Michigan: Servant Publications, 1993), p. 58

83 Leonard Ravenhill, *Why Revival Tarries* (Minneapolis, Minnesota: Bethany House Publishers, 1956), p. 83

84 Walter Wink, *Engaging the Powers* (Minneapolis, Minnesota: Fortress Press, 1992), p. 299

85   Ibid, p. 299

86   This outline was influenced by John Blanchard's exposition of James 5:16 in *Not Hearers Only* (London: Word Books, 1974), pp. 80-86.

87   Jack Deer, *Surprised by the Voice of God* (Grand Rapids, Michigan: Zondervan Publishing House, 1996) p 97-98.

88   Ravenhill, p. 51

89   Ibid, p. 82

90   Ibid, p. 23

91   Ibid, p. 24

92   Patrick Johnstone and Jason Mandryk *Operation World* (Carsilse, Cumbria: Paternoster Lifestyle, 2001), p. 8

93   "The State of the Unfinished Task" *Mission Frontier*, July-August 2010, 10.

94   Ibid, 10

95   Bread for the Hungry, Have Faith, End Hunger "The Faces of Hunger" http://www.bread.org/hunger/global/ (accessed September 11, 2010

96   Ibid, (accessed November 9, 2010)

97   Ravenhill p. 24

98   Selwyn Hughes, p. 55

99   Tommy Tenny, *The God Catchers* (Nashville, Tennessee: Thomas Nelson Publishers, 2000), p. 191

100 C. Peter Wagner, p. 70-71

101 Patrick Johnstone, *Operation World* (Carlisle, Cumbria: OM Publishing, 1993,1995), 337

102 Ibid, p. 337

103 Bill Bright, *The Coming Revival: America's Call to Fast, Pray and "Seek God's Face."* (Orlando, Florida: NewLife Publications, 1995), p. 79

104 Gary Tangeman *The Disciple Making Church in the Twenty-First Century* (Pennsylvania: Christian Literature Crusade, 1996), p. 202

105 http://www.jamaica-gleaner.com/gleaner/20060225/news/news6.html (accessed November 9, 2010)

106 http://www.jamaica-gleaner.com/gleaner/20060225/news/news6.html (accessed November 9, 2010)

CHAPTER FIVE

Hezekiah's Weakness: He Responded Inappropriately to the Blessings of God

107   William Wilson, 106

108   Ibid, p. 367

109   Ibid, p. 367

110   Ibid, p. 204

111   Joseph Gilmore, "He Leadeth Me," in *Praise! Our Songs and Hymns* (Grand Rapids, Michigan: Singspiraton, 1979), p. 364

112   Fanny Crosby, "All the Way my Saviour Leads Me," in *Praise! Our Songs and Hymns* (Grand Rapids, Michigan: Singspiration, 1979), p. 375.

113   Dottie Rambo, "Remind Me, Dear Lord," Copyright 1966 by Heart Warming Music. Assigned to Singspiration, a Division of Zondervan Corporation, 1981.

Works Cited

Alexander, David and Pat Alexander, *The Lion Handbook of the Bible*, Hertz: Lion Publishing, 1973.

Anderson, Neil and Charles Mylander. *Setting Your Church Free: A Biblical Plan to Help Your Church*. Ventura, California: Regal Books, 1994.

Blackaby, Henry and Claude King. *Experiencing God: Doing and Knowing the Will of God*. Nashville, Tennessee: LifeWay Press, 1990.

Blanchard, John, *Not Hearers Only* London: Word Books, 1974

Bowie, Richard. *Light For The Nations: A Biblical Theology Of Evangelisation*. Tanglin, Singapore: Haggai Centre For Leadership Studies, 1992.

Bright, Bill. *The Coming Revival: America's Call to Fast, Pray and "Seek God's Face."* Orlando, Florida: NewLife Publications, 1995

Bright, Bill. *The Transforming Power of Fasting and Prayer.* Orlando, Florida: New*Life* Publication, 1997

Bubeck, Mark. *The Adversary: The Christian Versus Demonic Activity.* Chicago: Moody Press, 1975

Bubeck, Mark. *Overcoming the Adversary: Warfare Praying Against Demonic Activity,* Chicago: Moody Press, 1984.

Coleman, Robert. *The Master Plan of Discipleship.* Grand Rapids, Michigan: Fleming H. Revell, 1987, 1988.

Cymbala, Jim. *Fresh Wind, Fresh Fire.* Grand Rapids, Michigan: Zondervan Publishers, 1997

Damazio, Frank. *Seasons of Revival: Understanding the Appointed Times of Spiritual Refreshing.* Portland, Oregon: BT Publishing, 1996

Deer, Jack. *Surprised by the Voice of God.* Grand Rapids, Michigan: Zondervan Publishing House, 1996

Dockery, David (ed.), *The Challenge of Postmodernism: An Evangelical Engagement.* Wheaton, Illinois: Victor Books, 1995

Evangelical Training Association. *Growing Toward Spiritual Maturity.* Wheaton, Illinois: Evangelical Training Association, 1988.

Fernando, Ajith. *Sharing the Truth in Love: How to Relate to People of Other Faiths.* Grand Rapids, Michigan: Discovery House Publishers, 2001

Gibbs, Eddie and Ian Coffey. *Church Next: Quantum Changes in Christian Ministry.* Downer's Grove, Illinois: Inter Varsity Press, 2000.

Hughes, Selwyn. *Revival: Times of Refreshing.* Lottbridge Drove: Kingsway Publications, 1984.

Johnstone, Patrick. *Operation World* Carlisle, Cumbria: OM Publishing, 1993,1995

Johnstone, Patrick and Jason Mandryk. *Operation World* Carlisle, Cumbria: Paternoster Lifestyle, 2001.

Katz, Arthur. *Apostolic Foundations: The Challenge of Living an Authentic Christian Life.* Minnesota: Burning Bush Publications, 1999

Kaiser, Walter, Jr. *Quest for Renewal: Personal Revival in the Old Testament.* Chicago: Moody Press, 1984

LaSor, William, David Hubbard and Frederic Bush, *Old Testament Survey.* Grand Rapids, Michigan: William B. Eerdmans Publishing Company, 1982

Malphurs, Aubrey. *Advanced Strategic Planning: A New Model For Church and Ministry Leaders.* Grand Rapids, Michigan: Baker Book House, 1999.

Miller, Madeleine S and J. Lane Miller, *Harper's Encyclopaedia of Bible Life*, eds. Boyce M. Bennett and David H. Scott. New York: Harper and Rowe Publishers, 1978

Morgan, Robert J. *Nelson's Complete Book of Stories, Illustrations and Quotes.* Nashville, Tennessee: Thomas Nelson Publishers, 2000.

Pfeiffer, Charles and Howard Vos and John Rea (eds.) *Wycliffe Bible Encyclopaedia* Chicago: Moody Press, 1975

Ravenhill, Leonard. *Why Revival Tarries.* Minneapolis, Minnesota: Bethany House Publishers, 1956.

Richardson, Rick. *Evangelism Outside the Box: New Ways to Help People Experience the Good News.* Downers Grove, Illinois: Inter-Varsity Press, 2000.

Smith, Ashley. *Emergence from Innocence: Religion, Theology and Development.* Mandeville: Eureka Press, 1991

Tangeman, Gary. *The Disciple Making Church in the Twenty-First Century.* Fort Washington, Pennsylvania: Christian Literature Crusade, 1996.

Taylor, William D. *Global Missiology For The Twenty First Century.* Grand Rapids, Michigan: Baker Book House, 2000

Tenny, Tommy. *The God Chasers.* Shippensburg, Pennsylvania: Destiny Image Publishers, 1999.

Tenny, Tommy. *The Daily Chase*. Shippensburg, Pennsylvania: Destiny Image Publishers, 2000.

Tenny, Tommy. *The God Catchers*. Nashville, Tennessee: Thomas Nelson Publishers, 2000.

Verwer, George. *Out of the Comport Zone*. Waynesboro, Georgia: Paternoster Publishing, 2000.

Vine, W. E and Merrill F. Unger and William White, *Vine's Complete Expository Dictionary of Old and New Testament Words*. Nashville, Tennessee: Thomas Nelson Publishers, 1985.

Wagner, C. Peter. *Prayer Shield*. Ventura, California: Regal Books, 1997

White, Tom. *Breaking Strongholds: How Spiritual Warfare Sets Captives Free*. Ann Arbor, Michigan: Servant Publications, 1993.

Wink, Walter. *Engaging the Powers*. Minneapolis, Minnesota: Fortress Press, 1992.

Wilson, William. *Old Testament Word Studies*. Grand Rapids, Michigan: Kregel Publications, 1978.

810.00

Eulalyn Clarke
Memorial Day
May 27th 2013